6. 80

Tides Of Empire

TIDES OF EMPIRE

Discursions on the Expansion of
Britain Overseas

Gerald S. Graham

McGill–Queen's University Press
Montreal and London 1972

This work has been published with the help
of a grant from the Harvey T. Reid Lectureship
Fund of Acadia University and a grant from
the J. B. Smallman Memorial Research Fund
for Research in Humanities and Social
Sciences of the University of Western
Ontario.

© McGill–Queen's University Press 1972
International Standard Book Number 0-7735-0137-1
Library of Congress Catalog Card Number 72-82242
Legal Deposit 3rd Quarter 1972

Design by Anthony Crouch

Printed in Canada

FOREWORD

The Reid Lectures were established in 1958 by Harvey T. Reid, B.A.(Acadia and Oxon), D.C.L.(Acadia), of St. Paul, Minnesota. His purpose was to bring to Acadia University, at least every second year, an eminent scholar or man of affairs to give a brief series of lectures on some important phase of history or political science. Dr. Reid, who is a former Rhodes Scholar for Nova Scotia, expressed a basic preference for a theme related to the British Commonwealth of Nations, but did not rigidly so restrict the lecturer.

The seventh series of the Reid Lectures was presented at Acadia University by Dr. Gerald S. Graham on 18, 19, and 20 March 1969. The three lectures were entitled "Colonies by Repulsion", "Colonies as Bases", and "Colonies in Retrospect". They have been expanded and incorporated in the present publication.

Born in Sudbury, Dr. Graham went to school in Madoc and Markham, Ontario, and is a graduate of Queen's University, where he received the M.A. in 1925. He attended the universities of Harvard, Cambridge, Berlin, and Freiburg-im-Breisgau, obtaining his Ph.D. from Cambridge in 1929. He was the recipient of a Queen's Travelling Fellowship to Harvard, the Sir George Parkin Scholarship to Cambridge, a Rockefeller Fellowship to Germany, and a Guggenheim Fellowship to the United States. He served with the R.C.N.V.R. from 1942 until the end of 1944. At the time of giving these lectures, Dr. Graham was the Rhodes Professor of Imperial History at King's College, University of London.

J. M. R. BEVERIDGE

President
ACADIA UNIVERSITY

PREFACE

The prescribed time-space for five public lectures devoted principally to British imperial expansion obviously compelled me to deal only with broad issues and special problems or aspects of Empire. I am aware that the British Empire did not expand either in "a fit of absence of mind" or in a vacuum. Yet empire-building over four centuries remained for most of the time on the periphery of European affairs. Apart from economic programmes, there were no constant colonial policies; nearly all the Western powers, including Britain, regarded their overseas territories as scarcely more than profitable side-shows. Nonetheless, until the end of the nineteenth century, the British Empire was generally within Whitehall's grasp. The lines of force that guided British colonial enterprise round the world radiated from London.

Two of the lectures (chaps. 3 and 4), have been influenced by recent research; two are based on books and articles published in the last twenty years, and the fifth, the epilogue, is essentially an impressionistic summary of my views on the past history and future prospects of the Commonwealth. A short lecture course on disparate themes cannot easily be transformed into a homogeneous treatise, and I can only ask indulgence for the lack of a unity which a proper book should possess.

I am greatly indebted for skilled advice and comment to Dr. A. J. Hanna, Professor D. B. Quinn, the late Commander J. H. Owen, R.N., Professor W. N. Medlicott, Professor Dennis Austin and Mr. W. G. Dodds. I also wish to thank my hosts, President J. M. R. Beveridge of Acadia University, Nova Scotia, and the members of his committee, in particular, Professor D. G. L. Fraser, for much warm hospitality. My sponsors at the University of Western Ontario have been equally generous, and I am grateful to the Department of History and especially to its Chairman, Professor C. A. Ruud, for allowing me to revise and expand the original three Reid lectures.

G.S.G.

Talbot College
The University of Western Ontario

CONTENTS

Foreword   vii

Preface   ix

CHAPTER

1   Colonies by Repulsion: The Force of
Religious Antipathies   1

2   The Expanding Empire of the Eighteenth
Century   23

3   Safeguarding the Sea Route to India
in the Nineteenth Century   45

4   Pax Britannica and the Balance of Power
in the Nineteenth Century   71

5   Retreat from Empire: A Retrospect   89

I COLONIES BY REPULSION

The Force of Religious Antipathies

The British Empire had its beginnings in the sixteenth century with the conquest of the Atlantic by the sailing ship, and its future was to depend on successful competition for the command of sea communications. Of course, successful colonization overseas depended on many things—on careful exploration of bases for settlement, on sufficient capital, on a steady inflow of suitable settlers. But however important these elements, the fact remains that colonies overseas could only be maintained and exploited by those nations possessing sufficient well-armed ships to guard and nourish them. The destiny of North America lay in the hands of that nation which could control the Atlantic with ships of war.

The possession of such sea power depended naturally on the talent, prosperity, and stability of the colonizing country; and at the time when Columbus drew back the curtain on a new, tropical world, England was singularly unfitted for colonizing adventures. Unlike the Norsemen, the English had no deep-rooted tradition of the sea. Apart from occasional expeditions to Iceland and Spain, and possibly the odd voyage to Africa or the Grand Banks, English maritime attentions had been largely confined to the Channel. Henry VII had given some encouragement to the Cabots, and their vague landfalls were recognized by the map-makers of Europe. After the Cabots' time other men sought out the coast of North America in search of treasure and a northwest route to the East. But the relatively small and impecunious England of Henry VIII and of Elizabeth, although one of the most stable nations in Europe, was not strong enough in the military sense to establish in the New World a continental base of operations capable of withstanding the opposition of her rivals of the Old.

Indeed, both French and English efforts at overseas exploration and colonization were little more than attempts to side-step Spanish claims and authority. Neither country was in a position to challenge the Spanish monopoly in the Caribbean; any experimental projects of empire had to be directed towards areas far enough away from Spanish territory to avoid armed conflict. As long, for example, as French settlements were confined to the Gulf and River St. Lawrence, some three thousand miles removed from the Caribbean, they had some chance of survival. Spain was not interested in the forbidding northland. Cartier's voyages between 1534 and 1542 caused scarcely more alarm than did the earlier expeditions of the Cabots. It was generally assumed that English or French colonies, whether clinging to the barren rocks of Newfoundland or the isolated banks of the St. Lawrence, would be feeble and therefore harmless.

Spanish colonial hegemony in the New World was not in question. As a consequence of Spanish naval superiority, the eastern coast of North America from Mexico to

Labrador remained throughout the sixteenth century un-
occupied by Europeans. English privateersmen might, in
the manner of Drake and Hawkins, harry the Spaniard—
and singe the Hapsburg beard—but to seek a foothold on
the North American seaboard without constant support
from home was to court disaster. As long as Spanish naval
power was sufficient to interrupt or cut the Atlantic communications of her European rivals, the claims of such
rivals to share the bounty of the New World were staked
on sufferance.

In consequence, English adventurers sought paths to
riches beyond the Spanish reach, and in the 1570s began the
serious search for a Northwest Passage to China. In the
course of penetrating the Arctic, Frobisher and Davis—
each made three voyages—were not simply seeking a
short-cut to Cathay; their preference for fog and ice was
based on a proper respect for Spanish power in both tem-
perate and tropical zones. When they failed to find a
northern route, there was no alternative for resolute men
but to go back to the mainland of North America.

In 1583 Humphrey Gilbert on his way to reconnoitre the
shores of New England (as subsequently called) stopped on
the coast of Newfoundland, and investigated the prospects
of a pilot colony. Newfoundland was forbidding, but at
least it was safe. After Gilbert's tragic death at sea, his half-
brother, Walter Raleigh, while he too thought in terms of
settlement, aimed at fixing a base which could also be used
for attacks on the power and wealth of Spain in the Caribbean. He proposed to link privateering with colonization,
but his impulsive efforts after 1584 to establish settlements
in and around Roanoke Island (in present-day North
Carolina) failed through ill-preparation and military
weakness.[1]

1. See D. B. Quinn, "The Failure of Raleigh's American Colonies"
in *Essays Presented to James Eadie Todd* (London, 1949), pp. 61–85; also,

Nearly twenty years were to elapse after the defeat of the Spanish Armada before the question of establishing a mainland colony was seriously considered in England. By that time, although the peak of her imperial hegemony had been passed, Spain was still a considerable power. Yet she was willing to make peace in 1604, a precarious reconciliation which encouraged the Virginia Company of London to adventure boldly in 1607, and send one of their expeditions to the southern Atlantic coast of North America. There, the Virginia colony at Jamestown put down roots and lived.[2]

The difficulties in the beginning were appalling—fevers, pneumonia, lack of proper food through lack of skills, and finally troubles with the Indians which threatened the extinction of the settlement. Up to this point, every English colony attempted north of Mexico had been a failure; for a time it seemed that the Virginia effort would collapse simply because of actual human casualties.

Despite the defeat of their Armada in 1588, the Spaniards were still powerful enough to extinguish the little colony before it found its feet. Indeed, Spanish reconnaissance vessels watched the infant struggles of Jamestown, and were happy to report growing weakness and debility.

Quinn, "Edward Hays, Liverpool Colonial Pioneer" in *Transactions of the Historical Society of Lancashire and Cheshire* (Liverpool, 1959), III, 32–9. As long as men and supplies were forthcoming from England, Raleigh's third colony (that of 1587, begun under the active leadership of John White) was temporarily secure against both Indians and Spanish, and seemed likely to survive. But when the emergency of 1588 forced the retention of every English ship in home waters, the settlement lost the support by which alone it could live. Not until 1590 was White able to return to Roanoke, only to find that the settlement had completely disappeared. See D. B. Quinn, ed., *The Roanoke Voyages, 1584–90*, 2 vols. (Cambridge, Hakluyt Society, 1955), I, 65–71.

2. See Philip L. Barbour, ed., *The Jamestown Voyages under the First Charter 1606–1609*, 2 vols. (Cambridge, Hakluyt Society, 1969), I.

Why not let the Indians and the fevers finish the job? In no way did the settlement endanger Spanish trade; there was no gold, no silver; England would soon tire of profitless colonization!

For ten years or so, Spanish forbearance was vital to survival. After that, what put the first English colony on its feet was neither Spanish goodwill nor English political wisdom, but tobacco smoke. Leaf tobacco seems to have been first grown in 1612 by a man called John Rolph; by 1619 tobacco plantations extended along the banks of the James River, both above and below Jamestown. The plantation system, first based on indentured white labour, had begun.

When the Virginia Company first announced its colonization plans, the export of paupers and felons came second on the list of objectives; profit-making was third. The propagation of the gospel came first. Admittedly, the wars of Elizabeth had linked national faith with national loyalty, and proselytization was, therefore, associated with imperial expansion. Obviously the natives of North America could only be converted if Englishmen possessed and occupied the land. The failure of the French to establish themselves on the coastline clearly indicated that God had reserved "the countries lying to the north of Florida ... to be reduced to civility by the English nation."[3] "Religion above all things," wrote Captain John Smith, who kept the colony alive during the first fearful days, "should move us ... to show our faith by our works in converting those poor savages to the knowledge of God, seeing what pains the Spanish take to bring them to their adulterated faith."[4]

3. See Quinn, "Edward Hayes, Liverpool Colonial Pioneer" in *Trans. Hist. Soc. of Lancashire and Cheshire*, III, 35.
4. On the influence of John Smith and other proponents of colonization, see Carl Bridenbaugh, *Vexed and Troubled Englishmen 1590–1642* (Clarendon, 1968), chap. XI, "The First Swarming of the English."

As Richard Hakluyt pointed out, while the Spanish had been busily converting "millions of infidells," Englishmen had done little but declaim pious intentions. In his *Discourse of Western Planting* (1584) this distinguished recorder of English maritime explorations noted that Huguenot ministers accompanied the short-lived French colony in Florida (1564), and that clergy from England went with Frobisher and Drake; "yet in very deed I was not able to name any one infidel by them converted."[5] English missions in North America showed none of the enthusiasm and pertinacity subsequently manifested by the Jesuits or the Recollets. Colonization was not linked seriously with conversion. There was little honest effort, as Hakluyt put it, to instil into the parched minds of the heathen "the swete and lively liquor of the Gospell." Trade not only overshadowed missionary work, it often ran counter to it. Antipathy to Spain and to Roman Catholicism was not sufficient to transform an obligation into a passion.

Yet religious protest became the powerful driving force that sent the Pilgrims of the *Mayflower* to Plymouth, and the Puritans to Massachusetts Bay. Suffering from the restrictions and tyrannies of a state church at home, Englishmen sought to escape into the freedom of the North American wilderness. Queen Elizabeth's church policy was indulgent enough to be called "comprehensive," but it provoked as much bitterness among extreme Protestants as among Roman Catholics; and later in her reign as a result of growing severities a movement of Congregationalists or Brownists sprang up. Robert Browne wrote his disturbing analysis of the Church and State relationship in 1582, and recommended that congregations should be self-governing. The congregation, he contended, derived its authority not from an established Church ruled by a

5. E. G. R. Taylor, ed., *The original Writings and Correspondence of the two Richard Hakluyts*, 2 vols. (London, Hakluyt Soc., 1935), II, 217.

corrupt hierarchy, but directly from God. Consequently, any group of true believers in association could constitute a Church of Christ by making a covenant with God and with each other. Politically speaking, this was to provide the basis for the famous Mayflower Compact of the Pilgrim Fathers. There were to be no bishops or prelates of any sort; ritual was to be simplified and based on sound evangelical doctrine.

These dissenters were not all bitterly uncompromising; they were willing to uphold the King's authority in all matters agreeable to God's word; in brief, they wanted liberty to worship as they pleased. But in so seeking, they found themselves acting against the laws of England. Hence a large group, its nucleus from Nottinghamshire, escaped across the North Sea in 1607-8 to Holland, where they found a toleration not obtainable under the early Stuarts. They were still English, but English exiles; consequently their leaders were soon pondering the prospect of emigration to North America where they might establish their church under the English flag. They sought a settlement with James I, and to do him justice he was willing to connive with them provided they carried on peaceably. These Pilgrims (as they were to be called) made a good bargain in their first dealing with the Virginia Company; indeed, the negotiations suggest a good deal of shrewd business sense.

With the patent on board, the *Mayflower* set sail from Southampton in early September 1620, and in November 101 passengers, men, women, and children, landed on Cape Cod. Fortunately, they did not, as originally intended, go to Guiana; English Caribbean plantations were bidding for Puritan emigration, and had the tropics received the first nonconformist immigration they might have engulfed it. As it happened, the landing on Plymouth Rock—if it was the Rock—lay outside Company territory, and in 1621 a new patent had to be secured. In the bitter cold of winter, which took toll of half the arrivals, the most remarkable experiment in the history of English colonization had its beginnings.

Plymouth was founded by what might be called the upper working class—humble folk, farmers, mechanics, craftsmen. Their standards of learning as well as their morals were not those of the governing classes; but some of their leaders were men of education—for example, William Brewster, a postmaster,[6] and William Bradford, who became their historian and second governor.

Bradford's history of the Plymouth Plantation with its moving account of "Why the Pilgrims left England for Holland" tells the whole human story of relentless determination and sacrifice.[7] Excerpts of this work, along with various pamphlets and relations published at the time, revealed to the English-speaking world the possibilities of establishing sectarian or semi-religious colonies in America. The humility with which most of them were written impresses one as genuine; these people were not a stiff-necked, sullenly narrow type. On the other hand, they did not intend to establish religious and political toleration as we know it. Anyone in Plymouth who wished to lead a normal life had to join the Congregational Church, which might be described as a kind of left-wing of Presbyterianism. This form of Puritanism had little direct connection with what we might call "self-governing democracy," apart from the energy derived from its rugged anticlericalism. The leaders aimed at a state purged of ecclesiastical autocrats and shielded by local congregations against the centralized power of any hierarchy such

6. James I once spent a night at the post-house in Scrooby, Nottinghamshire, and was so impressed by the hospitality that William Brewster received an increase in wages of two shillings a day; F. G. Kay, *Royal Mail: The Story of the Posts in England from the Time of Edward IV to the Present Day* (London, 1951), p. 22.

7. It was not published in full until 1856.

as bishops.[8] In short, the Pilgrims were as rigidly Puritan—if anything, more so in their discipline—as were the middle-class Englishmen who came to Massachusetts Bay under the leadership of John Winthrop in 1630.

When the English settlers began the colonization of North America, they simply established beachheads—one at Jamestown, Virginia, and another at Plymouth, Massachusetts. As Professor S. E. Morison has pointed out, until 1630 New England was anybody's country. The Pilgrims who landed at Plymouth Rock ten years earlier were too few and too remote to have leavened any communities hostile or indifferent to their point of view. The settlement of the Massachusetts Bay Colony had more widespread and substantial consequences; this ambitious project was to determine the fate of the northern Atlantic coastline as far as the Bay of Fundy and Acadia. Within ten years nearly twenty thousand Puritan immigrants were to arrive, and three offshoot colonies—Connecticut, Rhode Island, and New Haven—were to be founded "to contest with Massachusetts Bay in rivalry for divine favour and godly living."

Unlike Plymouth, Massachusetts had the advantage of being peopled, not merely by religious nonconformists, but by an enlightened and energetic society, headed by learned ministers and gentlemen trained in the arts of government. It was the age when the small gentry of England had come into their own; indeed some of the greatest names in the struggle against Charles I belong to that class—Eliot, Pym, Hampden, Cromwell. These were the founders of parliamentary ascendancy, and in their

8. See S. E. Morison, *The Intellectual Life of Colonial New England* (New York, 1956), chap. 1, p. 8, and T. J. Wertenbaker, *The Puritan Oligarchy* (New York, 1947), pp. 19–23; also G. D. Langdon, *Pilgrim Colony: A History of New Plymouth, 1620–1691* (New Haven and London, 1966).

devotion to liberty and in their wisdom they were head and shoulders above the men who made the French Revolution. In the struggle that was beginning between King and Parliament, many of them like the Pilgrims sought refuge overseas, and, had Charles I won the war, many more would have followed. Cromwell himself confessed that he would have joined the emigrants had Parliament failed to pass the Grand Remonstrance.

The intricate negotiations which eventually enabled the Puritans to get control of the Massachusetts Bay charter are not fully known. Suffice it to say, in 1623 a colonization company called the Dorchester Adventurers had bought the Pilgrims' right to a fishing station at Gloucester on Cape Anne, and started a settlement in 1624 under patent from the Council of New England. A similar series of small settlements took shape along the coast of Maine. The Cape Anne foundation was not a success, partly owing to the poor quality of the settlers; and when it began to break up, a reorganized association managed to secure another patent and in 1629 received a charter creating a corporation known as the Massachusetts Bay Company. As it happened, this charter was vulnerable; it did not specify either London or the New World as the site of Company headquarters. It did not state that a General Court Meeting had to be held in London; why not therefore in a colony free from all government interference except that of a King some 3,000 miles away? Consequently there occurred a unique event in the history of colonization —the migration overseas of an entire English Company, vested with the entire powers of local management.[9] At a time when other colonies, Spanish, French and Portuguese were being governed from Europe, the colony of Massachusetts Bay was literally governing itself.

9. See Bridenbaugh, *Vexed and Troubled Englishmen*, chap. XII, "The Puritan Hegira."

The charter which Governor Winthrop brought with him in 1630 not only protected the Colony from the close attentions of the English government, it also provided a notable precedent for American institutions. It was a written document with limits on the ruling authority. The vital feature was the annual election of governor and assistants, not by outside authority as in Virginia, but by the freemen voters in the Colony, who met four times a year as a General Court. It is well to note, however, that although the scope of Company government in Virginia was more restricted, its inhabitants enjoyed a more liberal democracy than those in New England. In Virginia, practically every landowner had a vote; in New England, because of the difficulty of coming up to Church requirements (freemen had to be communicants), it was only about one in five.

Politically and socially, the Massachusetts colony was not a democracy; to the extent that Puritan ministers controlled the civil government, it was a theocracy. And within this Holy Commonwealth, a rigorous church discipline was bound to lead, not only to strict regulation of manners, dress, and amusements, but to the severe treatment of those unwilling to abide by the rules. The very men who had fled from the harsh restrictions of the Church of England were themselves unwilling to tolerate variations in their own established form of worship. Roger Williams was a very holy man, with strong business instincts; he was banished and eventually helped to create Rhode Island as a refuge of oppressed dissidents. That pious and cussed gad-fly, Mrs. Anne Hutchinson, suffered the same fate. In 1636 the Reverend Thomas Hooker withdrew from the colony and, along with John Winthrop the younger, gave a start to the collection of settlements which in 1664 became the united colony of Connecticut.

Equality of all men was not a basic tenet of the Massachusetts constitution; the slavery of lawful captives was permitted, or, indeed, of any strangers willing to sell themselves. Climate and soil, not morality, explain the absence of plantation slavery in the north. Although it can scarcely be argued that the Puritans misapplied the scriptures, certain inhumanities in administration suggest a leaning towards Mosaic law; their principal error was to confuse crime with sin. On the other hand, they were probably more merciful in general outlook than any other group of colonists of the time. The death penalty was used far less freely than at home; there was no imprisonment for debt; civil marriage was legal, and on the whole women had a far better standing in law than in England. Probably the most odious phase of their history was the period which saw the persecution of Quakers and witches; to these wretched victims of the *Zeitgeist*, they were merciless. It is well to remember, however, that in England between 1647 and 1661 some 6,000 Quakers were put in prison, and nearly 500 suffered death by violence. In New England, three Quakers were executed during the 1650s; nineteen poor wretches were hanged for witchcraft in 1692.

In its beginnings, the New England theocracy was bigoted and sometimes tyrannous in policies and practices. Yet the Puritan form of Calvinism was in many ways peculiarly suitable for a pioneer society. The modern American philosophy of "making good" or "climbing to the top" owes much to the Calvinist creed. It was a grand illusion without which few would have dared to risk the suffering, the drudgery, and the self-imposed isolation of an alien and savage land. Men could best serve God through hard work, and those who were successful had a sense of having fulfilled some particular destiny. They belonged to the Elect, secure in the knowledge of their future salvation. The doctrine of the Elect, along with the strict moral code, helped to build the New England conscience. Of course, in its lowest form, such a doctrine could be translated into a mere taboo on pleasure, as subsequently applied by "Watch and Ward" societies. A leading authority on the mind and conscience of New England, the late Perry Miller, denied the conventional view that the Puritans were killjoys, arguing that religious austerity is not to be confused with British Victorianism.[10] Nonetheless, the designers of The Scarlet Letter frowned on May Day frolics as sources of immorality; and although the average Puritan no doubt detested cruelty to animals, cynical observers noted that he seemed less concerned about the baited bear than about the pleasure its sufferings afforded to the spectators.

Between 1620 and 1660, these New Englanders had an enormous amount of freedom to run their own affairs; the power of the king was never sure or persistent enough to make the colonists feel that they were ruled from England. In France or in Spain, Catholicism went with the colonists; there was no real change in the theological point of view. What was damnable in Spain was damnable in South America. But in the English colonies there was this difference. The English government could not enforce its rules and regulations as completely as in London. It was always difficult to apply religious conformity at a distance; the Law was far away. Variety was permitted in America; the Church of England was less necessary there. So we find the King conceding the existence of other religions: Congregationalists in New England; Roman Catholics in Maryland; Anglicans in Virginia and Quakers in Pennsylvania.

Colonial existence was forcing men in authority to be

10. See Perry Miller, *The New England Mind* (Cambridge, Mass., 1953); cf. G. L. Haskins, *Law and Authority in Early Massachusetts* (New York, 1960). See also David D. Hall, ed., *Puritanism in Seventeenth-Century Massachusetts* (American Problem Studies, New York, 1968), especially the Introduction: "Since the 1930s the revisionist interpretation has become the new orthodoxy"(p. 3); and Daniel J. Boorstin, *The Americans: The Colonial Experience* (New York and Toronto, 1958).

tolerant against their will; and colonial existence in North America involved natural forces of peculiar if not unique significance—for example, the wilderness. In England a heretic or nonconformist could not escape. The whole country could be included in the law. But in New England, no matter how harsh Massachusetts might be, the discontented or the disillusioned had only to cross the frontier to acquire their own brand of tolerance or intolerance. Thus, all around Massachusetts grew fresh settlements peopled by men who wanted freedom to worship in their own particular way.

In many respects a certain rigidity of faith and conduct is an advantage to pioneers. This world is shaped by extremists, not by moderates. The Puritans were extremists, and, at the dawn of English colonization in North America, an extreme Protestantism was not a disadvantage.[11] However narrow their religious views, the Puritans were men of independence, drive, and initiative. In many ways these tough, bigoted Christians were the pick of the English nation, men and women better fitted in body and spirit to create a commonwealth overseas than any similar group in the world. Their morality was fierce and, in organization, autocratic. Yet, with all the terrors of the moral law, there was stability of domestic life; they were fathers and mothers, not adventurers, striving to carve homes in the wilderness. And, although they who had been persecuted, persecuted in their turn, all the forces of frontier life pressed in the direction of tolerance and were to be accelerated by the battles and the eventual triumphs in Westminster.

By the time Pilgrims and Puritans had found their way to North America, Catholic persecution in England had

11. Admittedly, if compared with contemporary Scottish Presbyterians, or with some of the sects, particularly the Independents of the 1640–60 period, they might appear as moderates.

practically ceased, and emigration was not, therefore, a means of finding bodily security and religious freedom. On the other hand, heavy penalties for practising the faith remained on the statute book, and, although few were executed, priests were occasionally expelled from the country. After the end of the war with Spain (1603), the sword of Damocles still hung over Catholic heads, but it was held by a very strong thread. Nevertheless, it was there, and it is understandable that members of the Catholic aristocracy and country gentry should consider the possibility of an overseas refuge to which they could retire in the event of renewed attack.

George Calvert, who had been Secretary of State under James I for nearly six years, took advantage of the new spirit of toleration to declare himself a Roman Catholic in 1625. In the circumstances he was bound to surrender office under the Crown, but a grateful monarch made him Baron Baltimore in the Kingdom of Ireland, a title based on a minor holding in his Irish estate, which he had received as his share of confiscated O'Ferrall country in 1619.

But the new peer preferred to colonize overseas. He had already acquired a substantial grant in the Avalon Peninsula in southeast Newfoundland, and in 1628 made the big decision to move his family and retainers bag and baggage to the New World. Baltimore was determined to found a Catholic colony, and he might have succeeded had not an unusually severe winter shaken his faith in the amenities of the Island. So he turned to Virginia, where under mellower skies a Crown colony had already begun to prosper as a tobacco plantation.[12] Unhappily, the

12. Not all of Baltimore's associates and servants left Newfoundland in 1629. A few brave souls stayed to provide the nucleus of settlements at Ferryland and Petty Harbour which have had precarious but continuous existence to the present day.

I am particularly indebted to Professor David B. Quinn for letting

Virginians proved to be obdurately Anglican, and refused to admit him unless he took the oaths of allegiance and supremacy. Two more years were to elapse before he was given an estate of his own, north of Virginia beyond the Potomac River. It was called Maryland, and Baltimore intended that it should be a Catholic foundation under the Crown, where men who lived on sufferance in England might practise their religion without fear of persecution, and, in the event that the English penal laws should once again be enforced, a place of refuge and safety.

Baltimore died in April 1632, but his son, Cecilius, the second Baron, carried on his father's project. Unlike the Puritan rulers of Massachusetts, however, the Catholic patriarchs commanded by the Catholic Lord Proprietor and a Catholic governor were sensible enough to avoid any policy smacking of exclusiveness. Survival depended on Protestant support both from government at home and from vigorous settlers in America. Consequently, the first instructions issued in November 1633 for the plantation Maryland decreed that "they should suffer no Scandall, nor offence to be given to any of the Protestants, whereby any complaint may hereafter be made by them in Virginia or in England"; furthermore, that Governor and Commissioners "treat Protestants with such mildness and favour as Justice will permitt. And this to be observed at Land as well as at Sea."

In a curious way, a Catholic colony, born of antipathies, survived by discreet accommodation. In the interest of peace and political stability, toleration of Protestants was expedient, and in 1649, when Maryland acquired a legislature, this admission of tolerance was written into the statute book. Meanwhile, the Catholic colonists continued

---

me read in manuscript his essay: "English Catholics and America 1581–1633." The paragraphs dealing with Lord Baltimore's colonizing efforts in Newfoundland and Maryland are based on his work.

to enjoy a political status and privileges unattainable by Catholics within Great Britain until 1829. Indeed, within Britain the basic hostility to Catholicism remained; the fear and hatred of Spain which had been engendered during the early phases of Elizabeth's reign remained latent for years among a majority of the English population, and seem to have been most deep-seated among the Puritans.

Hatred of Spanish Catholicism undoubtedly inspired the Long Parliament to set up in 1649 a corporate society for the propagation of the Gospel in New England. This body had authority to acquire lands and to send out Protestant missionaries and teachers. But despite individual initiative and reorganization little was attempted in the way of Indian conversion, and less was accomplished. A few men like John Eliot learned Indian languages, and even made translations of the Bible into Indian dialects, but the overall results were trifling.[13] There was no purposeful dedication because, with individual exceptions, there was no Christian compassion.

On the frontier it was axiomatic that the only good Indian was a dead Indian; in England the Puritan view of the Spanish Catholic was similarly lacking in charity. The Puritan zealot like the Reformation buccaneer saw himself as champion of the forces of righteousness against anti-Christ. "God made them as stubble to our swords" was a doctrine that served for Spaniards as well as English Royalists, a doctrine that could be hideously distorted by the very simplicity of a Puritan faith. Oliver Cromwell was essentially a Puritan Elizabethan in his unshakable antagonism for Catholic Spain. Such unbending resolution was not simply a matter of believing in the rightness of this or that principle. Cromwell knew that whatever choice he made,

13. After the American Revolution the trust funds were used for the benefit of Indians in Canada, chiefly the Iroquois.

whatever he set his hand to, must be right. This form of mental rigidity (not unknown to my Presbyterian ancestors) could be extremely embarrassing to his colleagues and country when he was wrong. "I could not," he said before the battle of Naseby, "riding alone about my business, but smile out to God in praises, in assurance of victory, because God would, by things that are not, bring to naught things that are. Of which I had great assurance, and God did it." "Unhappily for him," wrote Macaulay, "he had no opportunity of displaying his admirable military talents except against the inhabitants of the British Isles."

This curiously confident leader who fulfilled the purpose of "God the all-terrible" in blood and suffering was once described, somewhat naively, as "perhaps the only Englishman who has ever understood in its full sense the word Empire."[14] One might add that he understood it like a Spaniard. There is little doubt that the Spanish conception of Empire was unconsciously absorbed by Cromwell. It is well to remember, however, that Cromwell could afford to be empire-minded. By the middle of the seventeenth century England had the power to create and to sustain colonies overseas; she was no longer dependent on the enterprise of private companies or the consequences of religious persecution. Moreover, Spanish power, except in alliance with France, no longer threatened either British security or English imperial aims. Cromwell must have recognized that the age of religious wars was over. He must have been aware that the rivalry of western European powers for the spoils of New Worlds would continue regardless of theological loyalties and affiliations. Indeed, his famous Navigation Act of 1651 was aimed principally at Dutch trade competition, and in the course of incompar-

14. H. E. Egerton, *A Short History of British Colonial Policy*, 6th ed. (London, 1920), p. 64.

ably bloody naval battles he fought and sometimes trounced the Dutch.

Nonetheless, he was still incapable of separating his English nationalism from a kind of Protestant fanaticism, and no human being is more ruthless than a frustrated zealot. "Nothing is more dangerous," remarked J. R. Seeley in his *Expansion of England*, "than Imperialism marching with an idea on its banner, and Protestantism was to our Emperor Oliver what the ideas of the Revolution were to Napoleon and his nephew."[15] Whether or not he saw dangers to English liberties and the English faith from the fading arms of imperial Spain is as much a problem for the psychiatrist as for the political historian. But whatever the background of his thinking, antipathy to Spain certainly lent blood and iron to his grim purposes. His Don Quixote-like challenge to Spain revealed less judgment than was ever displayed by any other Puritan leader in the Old World or the New. The war with Spain was unnecessary; it represented a kind of madness. Yet Cromwell found the ships, he got the men, and for a time he got the money too—not as a jingo, but as a chosen Instrument of God. "Why truly, your great Enemy is the Spaniard," he told Parliament as late as September 1656.[16]

"Providence," he told his Council in July 1654, "seemed to lead us" to the attack on the West Indies. This statement of Divine sanction may, of course, be interpreted to mean that even after the middle of the seventeenth century Spain remained the European power best worth plundering. Certainly the squadron that swept into the Caribbean in the spring of 1655 had greedy as well as pious intentions. Instructions to Admiral Penn and General Venables may have aimed at ousting anti-Christ to the greater glory of

15. *The Expansion of England* (London, 1888), p. 114.
16. S. C. Lomas, ed., *Letters and Speeches of Oliver Cromwell*, 3 vols. (London, 1904), II, 511.

God, but they were also concerned with benefiting English trade. Unfortunately, neither Penn nor Venables possessed Blake's military and naval talent. Suffering heavy rains and bad food, the ill-trained troops sickened with dysentery. The expedition failed to subdue San Domingo, and Jamaica was taken as a poor substitute.

Cromwell took an almost masochistic comfort in accepting the defeat as divine chastisement for sin. "Set up your banners in the name of Christ," he wrote Vice-Admiral Goodson at Jamaica, "for undoubtedly it is his cause. And let the reproach and shame that hath been for your sins, and through the misguidance of some, lift up your hearts to confidence in the Lord and for the redemption of his honour from men who attribute their success to their idols, the work of their own hands. . . . The Lord himself hath a controversy with your enemies; even with that Roman Babylon of which the Spaniard is the great under-propper. In this respect we fight the Lord's battles."[17]

Determined that English colonization in the Caribbean should stick, he attempted to divert population from North America, seeking to persuade the New Englanders "to remove themselves or such numbers of them as shall be thought convenient, out of these parts where they now are, to Jamaica." But even incoming settlers with no roots to lose refused to be tempted. Failing thus to check or at least to direct the westward-spreading tide of emigration, Cromwell turned to Ireland. His efforts to achieve a "final solution" of the Irish question by a brutal policy of apartheid and emigration failed. On the other hand, the forced transportation of some few thousand native Irishmen did rivet the English connection with Barbados.

17. Charles Firth, *Oliver Cromwell and the Rule of the Puritans in England* (London, reprint 1924), p. 403.

Jamaica was colonized chiefly by the surplus population of the other West Indian islands.

It has always been difficult to distinguish between Cromwell's religious and imperial economic aims. In a macabre fashion, they went hand in hand. Self-righteousness was combined with commercial cunning and imperial imagination. "Praise God and keep your powder dry" was undoubtedly a maxim of personal conduct as well as foreign policy, or as one of his officers succinctly put it: "All that look towards Zion should hold Christian communion—we have all the guns aboard."[18] The Lord who rendered the enemy "as stubble" to the Puritan sword may have had a hand in conquering one important overseas island, but, with the exception of Jamaica, English colonization in North America owed little or nothing to positive state exertion. "Charles I gave the New World to the Puritans by attempting to suppress them in the Old."[19] In like manner, Cromwell's imperialism, whatever the economic implications, was essentially a product of antipathies. He dreamed the same dreams and coveted the same material rewards as his hated Spanish imperialists. He was, in effect, a Puritan conquistador whose colonial thinking was founded on religious repulsion.[20]

---

18. C. V. Wedgwood, *Oliver Cromwell* (London, 1947), p. 125.

19. G. M. Trevelyan, *England under the Stuarts* (London, 1925), p. 324.

20. ". . . religion was an immense force in favour of making a British Empire; but it was a force which, in the case of the English in the sixteenth century, and to a large extent later also, operated more by repulsion than by attraction"; Sir Charles Lucas, *Religion, Colonising and Trade: The Driving Forces of the Old Empire* (London, 1930), p. 8.

2 THE EXPANDING EMPIRE OF THE EIGHTEENTH CENTURY

Less than five hundred years ago the boundaries of the western universe were shattered by inquisitive explorers who reached out over unknown waters and found strange lands on the other side of a globular earth. Although not realized at the time, the European struggle for power on the North and South American continents had begun when Columbus, by linking a New World to the Old in 1492, laid the foundations of the Spanish overseas empire. Five years later the ambit of European ambitions was once again widened when Vasco da Gama rounded the Cape of Good Hope, establishing a route to the East that has been followed to this day. Ranged along the Atlantic seaboard, Spain, Portugal, France, Holland, and England sought in turn to exploit the discoveries. The subsequent colonial rivalries of these western powers occupy no small part of modern history.

As competition for overseas wealth in terms of gold, silver, and important raw materials increased during the sixteenth century, European states had to revise their calculations on the sources of national power; age-old policies of continental conquest and territorial expansion were soon conflicting with new and inviting dreams of riches to be found in ancient and vulnerable empires over the horizon. In the past, territorial expansion, founded on military land force, had been the principal issue of European rivalry. In the new age of the sailing ship, the search for empires across the oceans gradually became an important supplementary pursuit. By the end of the sixteenth century it was obvious that the wealth of the New World as well as of Asia could be garnered only by those nations which possessed sufficient well-armed ships to transfer it. A new element, scarcely perceptible at first, was about to tilt the scales of the European balance—sea power.[1]

Spain had the advantage of a head start, but for reasons which economic historians have gone to some length to explain, she failed to develop a stable financial and administrative basis from which to exploit the power provided by overseas resources. Nonetheless, despite her decline as a major European state during the seventeenth century, her empire in Central and South America remained intact for a surprisingly long time. Remoteness from the main theatre of imperial rivalry northward of the Caribbean was the key to immunity. Consequently, successive Spanish governments were still able to monopolize the commerce of their increasingly resentful dominions. Discoveries of silver, gold, and diamonds brought settlers, soldiers, and administrators, but in the long run embittered natives and corrupt officials combined to break the mother

---

1. G. S. Graham, *Empire of the North Atlantic*, 2nd ed. (London and Toronto, 1958), p. 19.

country's monopoly by circumventing rigid regulations. Only in the second half of the eighteenth century did Spain's governors cautiously relax trade restrictions, and, like the equally harried Portuguese in Brazil, try unsuccessfully to eliminate abuses that were to pave the way, early in the nineteenth century, for armed revolt and the establishment of independent Latin American republics.

Meanwhile, in the years that followed the defeat of the Armada in 1588, a small, aggressive, and fiercely ambitious republic, recently relieved of its Spanish overlords, sought to share the bounty of distant lands. In Indonesian seas the Dutch ousted the enfeebled Portuguese, and took over the greater part of their empire. Holland proved to be far more businesslike in technological performance and colonial administration than Spain, but she had not the financial strength to maintain by force of arms a worldwide empire and survive as a European nation. Geography was against her. A small sea-borne state on the borders of France lacked the resources to maintain a first-class navy as well as an army sufficient to withstand the invading hordes of Louis XIV. By 1674 she had lost for a second time, and finally, her one strategic base in North America, New Amsterdam (New York). On the other hand, she was able to hold on sufferance until the end of the eighteenth century diminutive settlements at the Cape of Good Hope and in Ceylon. Her more significant East Indies possessions, as we shall see, were restored after the Napoleonic Wars, and remained intact until the Second World War of our own times.

The lessons of the bloody Anglo-Dutch wars in the second half of the seventeenth century were not lost on studious contemporaries. By the end of the century, strategic doctrines had begun to crystallize. The primary aim of naval warfare was no longer simply "the defence of the Kingdom," with pillage as a side-line, but the destruction of the enemy's fleets. By thus winning control of lines of sea communications, it was possible to prevent an enemy from moving his merchant ships (or warships) from one point to another without risk of capture. The possession of such power involved—to use the time-honoured phrase—"command of the sea." In a nutshell, this meant simply the effective command of all maritime routes that might be used by an enemy during war. This control could extend more or less around the world, or be related simply to waters (for example, the Mediterranean or the North Sea) adjacent to the respective territories of the belligerents.

In theory, however, the effect of naval supremacy was unlimited; as demonstrated in practice, the exercise of command of the sea in the eighteenth century permitted the expansion and sustenance of the scattered British Empire overseas. After all, unlike the land surface of the globe, the sea is one piece; and if the main enemy forces were broken or blockaded in harbour, British merchant ships could sail in reasonable security anywhere in the world, risking only the assaults of privateers or occasional raiding squadrons.

By the end of the seventeenth century, we are, therefore, at the beginning of a new age. The navy that defended overseas trade by seeking command of the sea was about to become—in the words of Lord Halifax (written in 1694)— "the life and soul of Government."[2] Essentially, Halifax was identifying expanding colonial commerce with national strength; and nearly half a century after his pronouncement, the French foreign minister, the duc de Choiseul, expressed the same principle at greater length when he wrote: "It is the colonies, trade, and in consequence, sea power, which must determine the balance of power upon the continent."[3]

2. Walter Raleigh, ed., *The Complete Works of George Savile, First Marquess of Halifax* (London, 1912), p. 175.
3. Quoted in Herbert Rosinski, "The Role of Sea Power in Global Warfare of the Future," *Brassey's Naval Annual, 1947* (London, 1947), p. 103.

With the opening of the eighteenth century the trading and financial interests had grasped this fundamental doctrine and were already, for their own benefit, propagating the argument that maritime commerce and naval power were indissoluble. The first round in the Hundred Years' War with France that was to decide the validity of this declaration of faith began in 1701 and continued to 1713. The War of the Spanish Succession, as it was called, was the first essentially "businessman's war" in modern history, waged quite as much to determine which European nation should possess the Spanish colonial trade, as which candidate should possess the Spanish Crown.[4] The sequel was a "businessman's peace" in 1713, an instrument of business insurance, which made handsome provision for Britain's commercial expansion overseas.

By the Treaty of Utrecht (1713) Britain was able to extend the network of naval bases which served her transoceanic communications. Along with the Hudson Bay territories, she got Newfoundland, with a reservation of French fishing rights on the northwest shore, Acadia (excluding Cape Breton island), St. Kitts in the West Indies, and two Mediterranean stepping-stones, Gibraltar and Minorca. And by forcing Spain to concede the infamous "asiento," she obtained the sole right to trade in slaves with Spanish America, thus laying the basis for her leadership in the slave trade until the end of the eighteenth century. Moreover, by establishing a naval ascendancy over her rivals in Western Europe, the new Britain, which the union with Scotland had brought into being in 1707, was in a position to make the world her commercial oyster.

The twenty-five years that followed the Treaty of Utrecht was outwardly a period of tranquillity so far as imperial developments were concerned. No new colonies

4. A. M. Wilson, *French Foreign Policy during the Administration of Cardinal Fleury 1726–1743* (Cambridge, Mass., 1936), p. 42.

were planted, and until the time of Cook, Wallis, and Carteret there was little British maritime exploration to record. It was a curious Indian summer which witnessed under the shelter of a "cease fire" the intense growth of Anglo-French rivalry. The explosion point came in October 1739, when Britain's declaration of war against Spain (the War of Jenkins' Ear) made renewed conflict with Spain's ally France almost unavoidable. It began as a businessmen's crusade. Inevitably, it was the merchants who formed the vanguard of citizen patriots demanding the destruction of the Spanish monopoly in revenge for Captain Jenkins' missing ear. The House of Commons must have been the scene of surging emotion when the Captain, holding up the bottle purportedly containing the lost ear, told his rapt audience that at the moment of amputation, he had offered up "his soul to God and his cause to his country."

When the War of Jenkins' Ear merged into the War of the Austrian Succession, British statesmen were for the moment too deeply immersed in European affairs to give much attention to imperial affairs. The fact that the first great battle in the second round of the "duel for empire" was fought far up the Rhine near the little village of Dettingen, in June 1743, seemed to confirm an earlier assumption that colonial rivalries should not be allowed to complicate major European policies.[5]

Indeed, despite the recognized association of colonial wealth and national power, overseas colonies remained on the periphery of British diplomacy. British governments were not interested in extending Anglo-Saxon dominion beyond reach of salt water. The British trade and navigation system had been developed through the years to

---

5. See L. M. Penson, *The Colonial Background of British Foreign Policy* (London, 1930), p. 15; Graham, *Empire of the North Atlantic*, pp. 112–15.

control an empire of commercial entrepôts, whether on the coasts of India and West Africa, or along the Atlantic seaboard of North America. There was no wish for conquests on land, because colonies counted only to the extent that they contributed to commerce with a minimum of overhead expenditure. According to good mercantilist logic, colonial commerce would be most cheaply secured by means of bases, outposts, or factories supplied and defended by ships of war; defence of overseas colonial trade was *not* to be linked with burdensome territorial acquisition.

The Treaty of Aix-la-Chapelle, although formally concluding the indecisive War of the Austrian Succession in 1748, was founded on a settlement too unstable to be lasting. In North America and in India there were all sorts of signs and incidents indicating that each side hoped to oust the other; there was a growing feeling that there was no room for both. In Canada, a string of feeble settlements along the St. Lawrence River had developed into a small but vigorous and nearly self-sustaining colony; and French ministers as well as French adventurers were bold enough to dream of overrunning North America as far west as the great plains and southward by the Mississippi to the Gulf of Mexico. It was a daring and magnificent conception of empire, first mooted by French explorers who talked of shutting the English forever behind the Appalachian mountain barrier. Likewise in India, French leaders like Dupleix showed imperial imagination far beyond their stolid rivals. Unhappily, neither in the East nor the West were sufficient French ships and men available to bring fantasy to life.

Some historians, including French scholars, have taken the view that if the ruling power in France had displayed sufficient inclination to support the ambition and enterprise of colonists and Company employees, French dominion would have been secured. The golden opportunity, they contend, was lost through lack of home interest in overseas affairs and the clash of personalities at court, which sometimes led to the betrayal of distinguished colonial governors and generals.

This argument is partly valid. The only real hope for the French empire overseas lay in putting maritime power and overseas colonization ahead of European ambitions, a course of action urged at times by some very able men in French councils. But this was asking a lot. Such a policy would have meant diverting heavy military expenditure to naval purposes, and for a continental country so bold an experiment was neither practical politics nor good economics. Having no protective moat like the English Channel, France had to be a strong military power for the sake of her own security. Of course she longed for a big navy and dreamed of a great overseas empire, but apart from intermittent bursts of enthusiasm, no French statesman was prepared to pay the price at the expense of *le sol de France*. With the exception of the War of American Independence, when a continental coalition gave her temporary superiority, France had to count on losing the war at sea.[6]

By contrast, Britain could afford to neglect her army and still remain a first-class power. An enemy might threaten communications, or attack an overseas colony, but as long as superiority at sea was maintained, the soil of Britain was rarely in danger, and provided there was no swopping of spoils at the peace table, the British Empire could expand with every victory.

In short, once British command of the sea had been effectively established, French footholds in North America

6. See Graham, *Empire of the North Atlantic*, pp. 109–12.

and in India were bound to be precarious. During the short years of truce after 1748, Britain maintained a comfortable superiority over both French and Spanish navies, with the additional advantage of unified command. By the beginning of the Seven Years' War in 1756 she had 130 ships of the line; France possessed 63, of which only 45 were in respectable condition; Spain could contribute 46, but most of these were in a sad state of repair.

As for bases, Britain had Bombay (then the best port in the East) and a number of good Atlantic ports, including New York, Boston, and Philadelphia. France held Cape Breton's Louisbourg and Quebec, but Quebec was far up the River St. Lawrence, and of little value as a base for operations. Similarly Madras, like other French harbours on the east coast of India, was useless as a harbour during the northeast monsoon. On the other hand, France possessed an army of 300,000 trained soldiers; the British peacetime army mustered only about 40,000 horse and foot. Moreover, the segmented and quarreling British colonies in North America had nothing to match French autocratic organization. In Canada, for example, all control was vested in a central authority with dictatorial power free from the influence of locally elected councils and civil officials.

It is proper to pay special attention to North America because, unlike India, where two commercial companies fought for supremacy, the contest was between rival settlers as well as rival European states. By comparison with the British Atlantic colonies, the population of the French colony was tiny; at the beginning of the eighteenth century scarcely more than 10,000 Frenchmen and women had settled on the banks of the St. Lawrence. Had Huguenots been forced, like the Puritans of New England, to take refuge in Canada (instead of being barred from that colony) French dreams might have stood a chance of fulfilment. Had a mere half of one per cent of the French population of some eighteen millions been persuaded to emigrate to Canada at the beginning of the eighteenth century, the colony would have gained the numerical strength and roots which alone could justify imperial policies of expansion overseas. Unhappily for France, twenty times as many English and Scots emigrants were packing themselves into the coastal strip east of the Appalachians. Against the weight of more than two millions, a colony of under 50,000 in 1756 could scarcely fulfil the designs of its explorers and governors. In the circumstances, the great French empire, stretching from the Gulf of Mexico to the valley of the St. Lawrence and Hudson Bay was little more than a paper option which the government in Paris had no chance of confirming. It is doubtful whether in modern history two less evenly matched maritime powers ever fought each other in a struggle for world empire.

Although fighting had been going on informally in America and in India for two years, the Seven Years' War did not begin officially until May 1756. In Europe two small countries, Britain and Prussia, faced the military power of two great continental states, Austria and France, and the opening phases suggested that they were doomed. Admiral Byng failed to relieve Minorca, and was executed "pour encourager les autres." Britain seemed to be losing control of the seas. In July 1757 the Duke of Cumberland surrendered with his whole army, and the forces of Frederick the Great of Prussia lay exposed to assault on both rear and flank.

Then occurred an extraordinary revolution in British morale and temper. Apprehensive about their own home security and aware of the sudden danger to their empire, the British people confided their fears to a leader of eccentric genius called William Pitt, who undertook not only to defeat France in Europe, but to smash the French empire overseas.

Pitt's assault on French possessions during the Seven Years' War was founded partly on a desire to relieve the Thirteen Colonies in North America from chronic frontier fighting on land and pillaging raids by sea, and predominantly on an almost fanatical urge to weaken France in Europe. By totally eliminating the French empire in every respect, Pitt intended to safeguard the traditional European balance of power. He was convinced that the destruction of the French empire, by severely damaging the French economy, was the key to Britain's home security. By depriving France of her overseas trade and its sources (which might mean territorial areas overseas) he was simultaneously adding what he believed might be decisive British weight to the scales of the European balance. Europe, and *not* empire, came first in his mind, because a favourable European balance meant national safety.

Before Admiral Mahan wrote his classic *Influence of Sea Power upon History*, an awareness of the implications of command of the sea was the prerogative of a very few statesmen and sailors. Pitt was one of this privileged group. Supremacy at sea, as he saw it, was essential to victory. Yet once operations were under way, he was slow to realize that in Canada and in India the striking force was the army, that local decisions had to be sought on land. It took him almost two years to weed out incompetent generals like Abercromby, and apply new methods in unfamiliar theatres of war. Indeed, Britain began offensive military campaigns for which she was unprepared. In 1757 she should have been capable of ending the struggle in two years; it dragged on for four.

The delay was partly owing to French defensive strategy. As long as France could win victories on the Continent, retain a hold on the Low Countries, or occupy Hanover, she could always enter the market of peace negotiations with valuable bargaining counters. What was lost on the high seas might be retrieved at the peace table. By avoiding operations likely to lead to a decision at sea and by keeping a "fleet in being," the French were able in the course of five campaigns to prevent Britain from conquering Canada, which under Pitt's direction had become one of the main objects of the war. Had they staked the issue on one fleet action during the first campaign and lost, Pitt would very probably have achieved his objective in half the time.

As it happened, the important victory on the Plains of Abraham following a two-year siege of Canada did not clinch the conquest. Wolfe's achievement was "glorious" because it came with all the drama of triumph and death after a long series of setbacks, but the honour which posterity has properly bestowed on a reckless and talented soldier has until recent times served to cloud the significance of Admiral Hawke's decisive victory at Quiberon Bay in November 1759. Not until then was the French power of intervention finally extinguished, and the way cleared for the relief of Quebec and the surrender of Montreal in the following year.

In similar fashion, Quiberon Bay settled the issue in India. For a time, François Dupleix, the enterprising governor of Pondicherry, seemed to have come close to success. By a system of princely alliances he had given France a complete ascendancy in southern India, and incidentally he had taught the British how a Company empire could be created by careful native diplomacy and small bodies of European-trained troops. But even if Dupleix had not been recalled in 1754, French power and influence were bound to fade. Clive's victory at Plassey in June 1757, which delivered Bengal to the English East India company, and Eyre Coote's decisive battle at Wandewash in January 1760, undoubtedly influenced the final result; but in last resort Hawke's destruction of the French fleet in Quiberon Bay settled the issue of European dominance in India. Henceforth no aid from France could be expected to help reverse the tide of British successes on land. Bereft of their dispirited native allies, the half-starved French forces struggled heroically but in vain. In defence of their trade and trading posts the British East India Company had been drawn into a costly war, only to find themselves after 1761 saddled with the responsibility of an unwanted oriental domain. The "empire of outposts" accessible by salt water had come to an end. The acquisition of Canada and huge areas of India witnessed the reluctant dawn of British territorial imperialism.

The Peace of Paris in February 1763 saw a disposition of vast and varied conquests that is without precedent in modern diplomatic history. Canada and all the territories east of the Mississippi became British, and in India, apart from a few very minor trading posts, France retained only two of her historical coastal settlements—Pondicherry and Chandernagore. But Britain refused to take Louisiana and the French West African settlements; she refused to exclude France from the Newfoundland fisheries, and re-stored her most prosperous sugar islands in the Caribbean.

Had Pitt been in power, he would have taken every-thing, and risked the world's censure; but his successors in Whitehall, eager to end the war, and possibly conscious of the dangers of a colonial monopoly, prescribed, in the interests of expedience, a far more moderate settlement. Notwithstanding, historians have been inclined to compare Bute, Bedford, and the peacemakers of Paris unfairly with the abstemious Castlereagh and Wellington at Vienna in 1814-15. This accusation of injudicious greed is based largely on the assumption that France and her allies, smart-ing under the humiliations of a vindictive peace treaty, had sought the first opportunity to take their revenge.

Such implacable enmity on the part of a defeated power has countless precedents in European history. What is unusual is the discovery by the vanquished of the right moment for reaping certain success. As it happened, the opportunity, when it came, was unique in British history, because a European balance of power essential to the safety of the United Kingdom disintegrated. In 1778 there was no Prussia, no Frederick the Great, to throw into the scales. Fifteen years after the conclusion of the Seven Years' War Great Britain faced a coalition of European powers, without a single ally, and the British Empire, enlarged and so beautifully consolidated in 1763, collapsed in ruins.

The disasters of the Seven Years' War had not been forgotten in France. Scarcely had the peace treaty been signed when French statesmen began to ponder ways and means of exploiting restlessness in Britain's transatlantic colonies. The minister of marine, Gabriel de Sartine, knew little about ships, but he had the good sense to surround himself with competent advisers, and under his driving leadership the French navy experienced a revival not unlike its short-lived resurrection in the seventeenth century under Louis XIV and Colbert. By 1778 France had some 60 ships of the line; by 1780, the number was 79; and in conjunction with the products of Spain's re-energized shipyards, she had a numerical advantage of about 30. For the first time since the battle of La Hogue (1692) the French navy was in a position to challenge British supremacy. The day of vengeance was close at hand.

In March 1778, France joined the war for American independence and was followed by Spain in April of the following year. As a result of this union, into which Holland was eventually pressed, Britain's European enemies gained for a fleeting but vital moment command of the sea in the west Atlantic and Caribbean theatre. The almost desultory action in Chesapeake Bay in October 1781 broke the British lines of sea communication and led to the surrender of General Cornwallis at Yorktown.

Chesapeake Bay was a trifling engagement as battles go, but because it signalled the ultimate victory of the Thirteen

Colonies and the collapse of the First British Empire, it demonstrated in chilling fashion that British command of the oceans was after all a very precarious monopoly. "If we had had a superior fleet in America," admitted the First Lord of the Admiralty, Lord Sandwich, "Lord Cornwallis would have been saved."[7] But such a concentration in North American waters was impossible, because in the year 1781 a resurgent France allied to Spain and Holland out-numbered Great Britain in home waters. At the time when Rear-Admiral Graves faced superior French forces off the North American coast, and Vice-Admiral Peter Parker confronted a substantial Spanish squadron in the neigh-bourhood of Jamaica, a weakened and badly neglected Channel fleet was preparing desperately to defend itself against a French-Spanish fleet, nearly twice its strength. Britain was threatened with defeat in European waters; and a colonial American war had turned into a fight for survival.

Without allied support on the Continent to divert French energies, the Royal Navy was not strong enough to ensure continuous control even in the Channel. Unless buttressed by effective alliances on the Continent, com-mand of the sea was a delusive concept.

But there is another consideration which emphasizes the limitations of naval power *per se*. Even if there had been no Yorktown—even if Britain had not temporarily lost command of the sea—it is most unlikely that the Mother Country could have quashed the American rebellion, and won the war. As long as British troops were regularly supplied from home, they might have kept their footholds in New York or Charleston; but the occupation of a few

7. The debate took place on 6 March 1782. See G. R. Barnes and J. H. Owen, eds., *Letters and Papers of John, Earl of Sandwich, First Lord of the Admiralty, 1771–1782*, 4 vols., 1932–38 (London, Navy Records Society) IV, 351; see also, Introduction, pp. 125–7; also Graham, *Empire of the North Atlantic*, chap. X, passim.

strategic segments on a coastline did not necessarily mean the subjugation of a vast territory that was largely in a position to support its own forces. So long as the British government insisted on putting down the rebellion, British forces were compelled to conduct major land campaigns at a serious geographical disadvantage. Since the American colonies were self-sufficient in food supplies, and only in part dependent on Europe for munitions and money, even a successful blockade of the French and Spanish ports could not have ended the struggle.

In other words, to suggest that only French intervention in North American waters could have won independence for the United States is an oversimplification. In one sense, of course, the argument has validity since the achievement of temporary command of the sea was decisive. The short-lived battle of Chesapeake Bay sealed independence, because it prevented the relief of Cornwallis's army, and led to its surrender. Yet if the French had not intervened in the North American theatre, Great Britain, bereft of allies, and occupied with three powerful enemies in other parts of the globe, could scarcely have found the resources and the men to subdue a quarter of a continent, three thousand miles away. It was not, therefore, administrative or military and naval ineptitude that was finally responsible for this humiliating defeat. The dominating factor was political isolation—the unprecedented absence of European allies. Without Frederick the Great on the continent, Britain would never have won so handsome an empire in 1763, and in similar fashion the Second British Empire of 1815 owed more than can be calculated to British allies who in the final years of the war against Napoleon prepared the way for Waterloo as the indispensable sequel to Trafalgar.

During the wars precipitated by the French Revolution, the British Empire was in no danger so long as Britain retained command of the sea, and the United States remained neutral. The comparative aloofness of the colonies and India from the main theatres of action, and not infrequently their indifference, are reflected in much of the official correspondence. During the first few years after 1793, France was rarely in a condition to carry the war overseas. The Revolution had disrupted naval morale; most of the officer class were driven from the Service as aristocrats or neo-aristocrats, and although the new recruits were good and sometimes fanatically zealous sailors, the experience and discipline were lacking. Moreover, the British blockade limited the import of naval stores from the Baltic, and many of the hundreds of hastily built ships showed dangerous faults soon after they were launched. All told, the French fleets which Howe, Nelson, and Collingwood defeated cannot be compared in quality of men and material with the fleets that sailed under d'Estaing, de Grasse, and Suffren during the War of American Independence. Unless the French had had the luck to win a battle as decisive as Trafalgar, their captains had not a chance in the world of ascending the St. Lawrence to Quebec, or taking Bombay by assault from the sea.

Moreover, the strategic situation had changed since Pitt's day. France was no longer required to expend energy in North America, but she had neither the capacity nor the opportunity to concentrate a powerful squadron in the Indian Ocean. Admittedly, she possessed one strategic base, Mauritius (Ile de France), on the way to India, and was able to compel her conscripted ally Holland to allow the use of the Cape of Good Hope station, as well as Trincomalee harbour in Ceylon. But even before these bases fell to the British navy, they were little used except by privateers. With the French ports of Brest and Toulon carefully guarded by blockading forces, there was little need for Britain to detach ships-of-the-line for overseas duty. Occasional hit-and-run forays and perfunctory clashes had no lasting effect on the conduct or course of the war. Decisive battles in the main European theatre—Cape St. Vincent, the Nile, Camperdown, and finally Trafalgar—extinguished any hopes France might have held of regaining power and possessions in North America and India.

A short-lived threat to the British Empire developed in June 1812, when Napoleon invaded Russia, and when, in the same month, the United States declared war on Britain and prepared to invade Canada. The acquisition of that colony, Thomas Jefferson had declared, was not likely to be more than a matter of marching; but off the Atlantic coast the situation was far less hopeful. With little beyond a scratch force of frigates, sloops, and gunboats, Americans were to suffer all the humiliations which lack of preparation and consequent defensive warfare invites, and which only the brilliant performance of individual commanders helped to redeem. The struggle for the Great Lakes developed into a shipbuilders' race within a self-contained area of operations where the superiority of the Royal Navy could not manifest itself. But the decisive theatre remained in the Atlantic, and only a battle fleet could have secured American coasts against attack by a naval power. In the long run, American seaborne commerce was whittled away by superior forces with devastating effects on the economic life of the Republic. On 14 December 1814 a war of expansion which had turned into a defensive struggle for existing boundaries was brought to an official close by the Peace of Ghent.[8]

Six months later, as a consequence of the downfall of Napoleon at Waterloo in June 1815, Britain confirmed a global predominance that was unique in history. Victory

---

8. Two weeks after peace had been concluded, a reinforced American army under Andrew Jackson repulsed with heavy losses a British force at New Orleans.

over France had transformed an empire originally based on control of the North Atlantic into one whose colonial bases encircled the earth, and whose centre of gravity was moving steadily towards the Indian Ocean. The total number of overseas colonies had grown from twenty-six to forty-three; and that number might have been vastly increased had Lord Castlereagh not insisted on confining acquisitions to ports and bases. Mindful of the lessons of the American Revolution, the British foreign secretary was anxious to avoid exposing his country to the dangers of a future *revanche* assault by jealous and resentful European powers.[9]

Yet British gains, although less in acreage, were of far greater strategic value for an expanding commercial and industrial power than those obtained in 1763. Gibraltar and Malta gave Britain tactical command of the western Mediterranean, while a protectorate over the Ionian Islands provided at least an observation post overlooking the Isthmus of Suez and the Red Sea route to India. By taking the Cape of Good Hope and Ceylon from the Dutch, and Mauritius from the French, she was able, with the addition of St. Helena and Ascension, to service the longer and safer road to the east. The acquisition of Trinidad, Tobago, and St. Lucia and the former Dutch colonies of Demerara and Essequibo provided further useful bases in the Caribbean. Fortified by technical revolutions unavailable to nations on a blockaded and war-torn Continent, industrial Britain towered over Europe. Her world position, in the military as well as the economic sense, seemed unassailable.

Meanwhile, France was held in decent restraint under

9. See C. K. Webster, *The Foreign Policy of Castlereagh, 1812–1815* (London, 1931), pp. 195 (Memorandum on the Maritime Peace) and 272–3, 491; also, by same, *British Diplomacy 1813–1815* (London, 1921), 127.

the auspices of the Holy Alliance. Until 1818 an occupation force of 200,000 men camped on French soil, and the state was condemned to pay 1,500 millions tribute. But damages inflicted on the national economy by war were more devastating than any indemnity. Two foreign invasions had cost France a million dead, and an estimated 1,500 millions of raw materials, manufactures, equipment, and livestock. Her merchant marine was negligible and her naval strength had been reduced to a shadow. Between 1793 and 1815 she had lost some hundred ships-of-the-line and more than 150 frigates. France was in no position for many years to come to challenge the overwhelming predominance of her former rival.

In 1815 little remained of her old empire except Senegal in West Africa, Martinique, and Guadeloupe in the West Indies, and a few isolated settlements in India—Chandernagore, north of Calcutta, Pondicherry, and Karikal on the Coromandel Coast—and the small island of Bourbon, safely anchored in the shadow of conquered Mauritius. These existed on sufferance—pinpoints of trade rather than bastions of power.

On the other hand, Holland was allowed to rebuild her shattered East Indies empire. In challenging the merchant interest by this positive act of appeasement Lord Castlereagh was simply maintaining Britain's traditional "balance of power" policy on the Continent. A friendly, independent, and strong Dutch state would provide, it was hoped, a barrier against the future designs of a revived and ambitious France. But apart from Holland, the beneficiary of European power politics, the pioneers of adventure and expansion in the East had dropped out in the centuries-long struggle for empire. Owing partly to traditional English friendship, the Portuguese maintained nominal control over three microscopic dots on the west coast of India—Goa, Damão, and Diu; and south of Cape Delgado on the east coast of Africa they clung obstinately to their anaemic and almost bankrupt colony of Moçambique—a loosely ruled strip of river-mouth settlements that stretched as far as Delagoa Bay. Equally precarious was Spain's footing in the Philippine Islands on the end of the China Sea. Manila, on the barely conquered and uneasy island of Luconia depended for its existence on annual subsidies from Mexico.[10]

All told, within the huge quadrilateral that extended roughly from the Cape of Good Hope to the Red Sea, eastward to the Malay Peninsula, across the Indonesian Archipelago to the northern shores of Australia, and thence back to the Cape, no European rival threatened British hegemony. Within this landlocked enclosure, Britain had established the nucleus of an informal commercial empire that was already reaching out to South America, China, and the islands of the Pacific.

10. See C. N. Parkinson, *War in the Eastern Seas, 1793–1815* (London, 1954), pp. 39–43.

3 SAFEGUARDING THE SEA ROUTE TO INDIA IN THE NINETEENTH CENTURY

By the end of the eighteenth century British India was more than a collection of coastal trading posts. The giant peninsula projecting a thousand miles into the Indian Ocean belonged to another world, like Marco Polo's China—a fabled world of spikenard and cloves, pearls and pagodas, unicorns and elephants, flowering silks and shimmering odalisques. It had become the citadel and principal headquarters of British dominion in the eastern seas. It was the strategic centre of a vast commercial network that included the Straits Settlements, the Indonesian archipelago, China, and Australia on the one hand, and on the other, Persia, Arabia, Egypt, and East Africa. A Company project initiated at the beginning of the seventeenth century with the establishment of a few trading ports had grown into an elaborate organization of trade, finance, and government based on London.[1] In the words of the French economist, Baron Charles Dupin: "From the banks of the Indus to the frontiers of China—from the mouths of the Ganges to the mountains of Thibet; all acknowledge the sway of a mercantile company shut up in a narrow street in the city of London!"[2]

In the sixteenth century, a monopoly of the Indonesian spice trade, enforced by naval supremacy, had been the simple policy of the Portuguese. Under the Dutch in the seventeenth century, but chiefly in the eighteenth century under the British, this traffic had expanded to include Indian products such as jute, indigo, raw cotton, hemp, and wheat, in return for steadily increasing shipments of cotton textiles, and eventually, during the nineteenth century, of the iron and other manufactures of England's factory age—the materials for railways, bridges, and harbour installations. Through all the changes, from the first cotton samples to the large-scale exports of capital and heavy equipment, India's economy became increasingly dependent on Europe, and almost completely associated with maritime carriage. Indeed, the portentous fact of modern Indian history is India's dependence on the sea. From the sixteenth century onwards, her political future was determined at sea, for it was easy access around the Cape that originally invited European conquest.

Physical geography prescribed that India should become an insular rather than a continental state. The very nature

1. See G. S. Graham, *The Politics of Naval Supremacy* (Cambridge, 1965), pp. 43-4.
2. *The Commercial Power of Great Britain* (originally published in Paris in 1821), introduction to the English edition, 2 vols. (London, 1825), I, v.

of India's frontiers made communication by land tedious and difficult. This is not to deny the strategic and commercial importance of the historic mountain passes. For centuries the Asian invader had found convenient loopholes to the northwest and the northeast. The mountain barriers of Afghanistan and the Himalayas were equally penetrable to the enterprising merchant. But once the shattered empire of the Moguls had succumbed to the European conqueror, the sailing ship became the chief medium of trade and influence throughout the Indian Ocean and beyond. Indian economic life and commerce were tied, not to Asia but to Europe, by means of the long sea track around the Cape of Good Hope. By the end of the Seven Years' War, the Indian Ocean had become a European—and for all practical purposes—a "British lake."[3]

For many generations England had maintained squadrons in the Mediterranean and managed to keep precarious control over the overland road to India across the isthmus to the Red Sea. But this portage route was affected by every shift in the European balance of power, as well as by the stubborn barriers of Islam.[4] After 1704 Britain had the benefit of a base at Gibraltar and subsequently at Malta, but no squadron based on these fortified harbours could guarantee the Mediterranean corridor against a sudden conjunction of enemy forces. For a nation possessing a general naval superiority, direct ocean communications with India were far less vulnerable; the all-sea passage around the Cape of Good Hope (which Vasco Da Gama

3. Admittedly this comfortable supremacy was challenged twenty years later by the great French Admiral Suffren.

4. Following the Arab conquest of Egypt all routes to the East from the Mediterranean had fallen under Mameluke control, and so remained until the Portuguese, from bases at Goa and at Ormuz in the Persian Gulf, were able to block most of the Egyptian-Venetian trade that had continued, even after the fall of Constantinople in 1453.

had traced in 1496–7) remained the most reliable road to the East.

Yet even the Cape route could be cut in time of war. To guard against this danger the approaches to the English Channel had to be closely patrolled, as Lord Anson had demonstrated, by use of a highly disciplined Western Squadron.[5] Such forces frequently acted as convoy escorts as well as scouts; indeed, the squadron of western Channel cruisers had frequently to be stretched to include St. Helena, the final rendezvous for homeward bound convoys from India. More distant areas of converging trade lanes were almost equally susceptible to enemy interference: for example, the waters off the Agulhas Bank adjoining the Cape of Good Hope, and the approaches to India proper, in particular the approaches to Bombay, Calcutta, and Madras. In such focal sea areas, where enemy raiders were likely to concentrate in time of war, it was necessary to maintain squadrons or detachments, whose strength varied according to domestic political exigencies and the changing state of international combinations. History has shown the far-reaching influence of small squadrons of small ships in distant waters. In the eighteenth century as in the nineteenth, the cry from the overseas stations for more sloops and frigates was constant—from the Cape to stop the slavers, from the West Indies to fight the pirates, from the East Indies and China stations to guard the trade against the privateers.[6]

5. Anson did not invent the Western Squadron; it had been well-established by the middle of Queen Anne's War, although then known as the Sounding's Squadron. See J. H. Owen, *The Navy in Queen Anne's Reign, 1702–1708* (Cambridge, 1938) pp. 68–9.

6. In 1914 the famous German cruiser, *Emden*, was not the first to cut into the trade of the Indian Ocean, and the explanation of her success as well as her long immunity was the lack of adequate ships of sufficient strength to convoy Allied shipping. Between 10 September and 9 November the *Emden* bombarded Madras and engaged highly successfully in commerce-destroying until run down and sunk at Cocos Island.

For the sake of efficient maintenance, overseas station squadrons required bases to which they could resort at convenient intervals for provisions and water, repair and refit. The outward journey by sail from the English Channel took months not weeks, and ships on station often required repairs beyond the capacities of ships' companies and the indispensable hulk or repair ship.[7] Similarly, bases provided depots for vital naval stores, and, after the middle of the nineteenth century, for the even more vital commodity, coal. Moreover, in hot climates refreshment in terms of recreation, food (especially fresh vegetables), and hospital care, was important. A base which could not supply its local squadron with provisions as well as the materials of war lost its *raison d'être*; strategically it might hold a position which popular journalists as well as admirals called a "key"—almost every base in the world was sooner or later called a key to something or other; but, as Admiral Sir Herbert Richmond pointed out, once it failed to fulfil its function as a sustainer it became in reality "of no more importance than a sentry box without a sentry."[8]

No base, however well garrisoned and fortified, was capable of indefinite self-support; indeed, it could be said to be almost constantly exposed, because no squadron was expected to defend a base at the expense of the primary task—the maintenance of sea communication. The object of the base was to enable the local or station squadron by means of repair, refit, and supply facilities, to retain its efficiency as guardian of neighbouring sea lanes. The base was there for the sake of the ships. The ships were *not* there for the sake of the base.[9] A naval base has never commanded the sea beyond the range of its own guns, and if the ships

---

7. At the beginning of the nineteenth century, the traditional operation of careening to clean the ship's bottom still continued, but a disabled vessel in serious need of refit required a dock.

8. *The Navy in India, 1763–1783* (London, 1931), p. 123.

9. J. R. Thursfield, *Naval Warfare* (Cambridge, 1913), p. 138.

were lacking, it became merely a hostage in the hands of a superior enemy which could cut its connections with the outside world, wear it down, and occupy it, as the British did twice at Louisbourg in 1745 and 1758. Superior sea power usually guaranteed ultimate possession; on the other hand, "hit and run" raiders were frequently in a position to inflict heavy damage on shore installations and civilian property. More than once in the West Indies or at Newfoundland, to take obvious examples, raiding forces either evaded or defeated the local squadron, and the destruction was always considerable. In Hudson Bay both French and British forts had at various times fallen to diminutive forces from the sea.

Before the Napoleonic wars Britain had, apart from St. Helena,[10] no bases of repair or refreshment of her own to watch and sustain the sea route to India more than 11,000 miles away. By the end of the war, she was in permanent possession of the Cape of Good Hope, Mauritius (the French Ile de France), and Ceylon with its harbours at Galle and Trincomalee. Until well into the second half of the nineteenth century, Cape Town was the most important of these bases, the only port in fact that was visited with regularity by ships travelling from the East. Its commanding strategical position is obvious on any map—the low point on an inverted triangle halfway between Europe and India. A voyage to or from England might take eight weeks, or three months at the worst; from the Cape to the Coromandel and Malabar coasts of India, or return, a matter of six weeks or three months depending on a favourable monsoon.

During the greater part of the eighteenth century the Admiralty had worried little about the Dutch colony at

10. Acquired by the East India Company in 1673, St. Helena became a Crown Colony in 1834.

the Cape of Good Hope. As long as there was peace or as long as Holland remained friendly, Dutch hospitality to needy British men-of-war or merchant ships could be taken for granted. But as soon as the United Provinces in 1780 were dragged into the Continental coalition that left Britain without a single ally to fight the War of American Independence, the Cape became a potentially menacing enemy base, and its capture essential to the security of India, and the serenity of the East India Company. No fleet, the Directors of the Company pointed out in October 1781, could possibly sail to or return from India even in peace time without touching at some place for refreshment, and the only remaining Atlantic refuge was the uninviting island of St. Helena.[11]

Even in peacetime, St. Helena could scarcely provide sufficient food for the homecoming ships which made their way up the west coast of Africa. In wartime it was dependent on supply from the Cape, and if the Cape were lost, St. Helena, it was assumed, might as well be written off. More precisely, if the French took the Cape from the Dutch, they were in a position to threaten, if not to control, the sea route to India.[12]

Consequently, when war broke out between France and Britain in February 1793, the first concern of the East India Company was the fate of this strategic halfway house should Holland again fall into the hands of the French. By flooding their countryside the Dutch government made a determined effort to block the invader, but during the severe winter of 1794-5 the barrier waters froze solid,

---

11. See Richmond, *Navy in India*, app. VI, pp. 414-17.
12. Or to put the argument in reverse—if the British expedition of 1781 had succeeded in taking the Cape from the Dutch, Admiral Suffren, as Richmond has remarked, "could not have shaken the existence of the Empire in India [as he did] in 1782 and 1783"; ibid., p. 126.

providing easy access for the French army of the North, which rapidly overran the country, defeating the combined Dutch, English, and Hanoverian forces that stood in the way.

Once again an anxious government was reminded of the Cape's close military association with India.[13] Energized by the appeals of Sir Francis Baring, chairman of the East India Company, Henry Dundas, secretary of state for war, sought the views of an experienced sailor, Captain John Blankett, who had served for some years in Indian waters.[14] Blankett had no reservations: the Cape in British hands would act as a check on France's important naval base in the Indian Ocean, Ile de France, which if supplied by the Cape, would become "a nest of pirates, secure and unattackable amongst their own rocks." And he added: "Whatever tends to give France the means of obtaining a footing in India is of consequence to us to prevent. It would be idle in me to say anything more to point out the consequence of the Cape than to say that what was a feather in the hands of Holland, will become a sword in the hands of France."[15] If for no other reason, as Baring pointed out to Dundas, the Cape should be occupied simply to prevent the French from taking it. It would be an expensive acquisition; as a colony it was useless, since it produced

13. In the opinion of the Governor-General of Bengal (Lord Mornington), writing in 1800, the Cape of Good Hope was not only a vital outpost of the Indian Empire, it was "a depot from which seasoned troops may suddenly be drawn for the defence of our possessions in the East in any emergency that may arise"; *The Spencer Papers*, ed. H. W. Richmond (London, Navy Records Society, LIX), IV (1924), 163.

14. He was made commodore of the Cape squadron in advance of the surrender of 1795, and appointed rear-admiral in 1799. He died in 1801.

15. *The Keith Papers: Selected from the Letters and Papers of Admiral Viscount Keith*, ed. W. G. Perrin (London, Navy Records Society, LXII), I (1927), 214.

nothing of value in the way of exports. On the other hand, he continued: "It commands the passage to and from India as effectually as Gibraltar doth the Mediterranean."[16]

Baring's appeal was answered in September 1795, when the Cape base surrendered to British forces, and was held, despite the efforts of a Dutch squadron in the following year to regain it.[17] News of the seizure of the base reached London towards the end of November 1795, and Dundas, who had doggedly favoured a colonial and maritime rather than a continental strategy, hastened to take credit for the coup: "The instant the French became possessed of Holland [he told the House of Commons] the idea occurred to him to get possession of the Cape of Good Hope. Whether Government would under any circumstances give up that valuable acquisition was a point upon which he should not give an opinion, except merely to say that it would not be given up without an ample compensation."[18]

Meanwhile, immediate efforts were made to bring an end to hostilities which even Nelson's victories rendered scarcely palatable. Lord Malmesbury was sent to Paris to find out if the French were equally weary of war and anxious for peace. He reported that in the course of conversations with the French plenipotentiary in Paris on 20 December 1795, he had told M. Delacroix that "what His Majesty would require would be possessions and settlements which would not add either to the wealth or power of our Indian dominion, but only tend to secure to us their safe and unmolested possession. You mean by this, said M. Delacroix, the Cape and Trincomale." Following

16. *Keith Papers*, I (12 January 1795), 210.
17. The British naval force was commanded by Rear-Admiral George Keith Elphinstone, created Baron Keith in 1797 and Viscoun in 1814. Blankett was his second in command during the operations.
18. *Keith Papers*, I (Speech in the House of Commons, 9 December 1795), 230.

a rather laboured disquisition on the value of the Cape of Good Hope as one of the most fertile and productive colonies in the East, the Frenchman added: "If you are masters of the Cape and Trincomale, we shall hold all our settlements in India, and the Islands of France and Bourbon, entirely at the tenure of your will and pleasure; they will be ours only as long as you choose we should retain them. You will be sole masters in India, and we shall be entirely dependent upon you." This sombre admission led Lord Malmesbury to offer, perhaps a little unctuously, Whitehall's enduring cliché: "I repeated to him, that it was as a means of defence, not of offence ... and that if the matter was fairly and dispassionately discussed he would find that they afforded us a great additional security, but no additional power of attack, even if we were disposed to disturb the peace of that part of the world."[19] Despite the determined casuistry of official pronouncements even up to recent times, the two concepts, offence and defence, cannot within the maritime context be separated.

Nearly six years elapsed before these frustrating conversations and negotiations were concluded. On 27 March 1802, by the sixth article of the Treaty of Peace signed at Amiens, the Cape of Good Hope was handed over not to France, nor to the United Provinces of the Netherlands, but to the Batavian Republic, which did not exist before the war, and which at no time during the war exercised sovereignty over the Cape. For Britain, it was a most unsatisfactory settlement, which the former prime minister, William Pitt, deeply resented.[20] Unlike Dundas, he did not contend that it had been "a most successful war," but he

19. *Keith Papers*, I, 233.
20. Pitt to Lord Spencer (First Lord of the Admiralty), 1 October 1801; *Spencer Papers*, IV, 304. Pitt had resigned office on 14 March 1801, but agreed to support the Addington Administration in the House of Commons. He resumed the leadership on 10 May 1804.

spoke as the party politician when he asserted that "our concessions, though great, appear a sacrifice to good faith and generosity, rather than the effect of timidity and weakness."[21]

In surrendering the Cape, the British government was not bargaining from strength; it was reacting from weariness, accentuated by gloomy estimates of the costs of a war that gave little or no promise of returns. Nonetheless, the Addington ministry faced an agonizing dilemma which was scarcely resolved by the partisan oratory of sailors like Nelson and St. Vincent, who argued that with the introduction of coppered hulls towards the end of the eighteenth century the Cape had lost much of its value as a refitting station. With the development of new techniques, Cape Town (as Nelson told the Lords) had become little more than "a pleasant tavern on the passage" whose temptations often interrupted a quick non-stop passage to Bombay.[22] Fortified by the judgments of professionals, Pitt had little difficulty in defending the transaction as an act of expediency. "If we could not retain the Cape without continuing the war," he told the Commons, "then the ministers [Addington and Hawkesbury] had acted wisely in giving it up on the terms they had, because in point of value, it was inferior to Ceylon and Trinidad."[23] In brief, the Cabinet were anxious to bring an end to an expensive war; this happy conclusion could only be achieved by surrendering a base, which, whatever its strategic value, was likely to prove in itself a costly administrative burden. If a choice had to be made, better the Cape should be returned than Ceylon.

21. Ibid., pp. 304–5.
22. Debate in the House of Lords on the Preliminaries of Peace, 3 November 1801; *Parliamentary History of England* (London, 1820), XXXVI, 185.
23. *Speeches of the Rt. Hon. William Pitt in the House of Commons*, 4 vols. (London, 1806), 3 November 1801, IV, 203–4.

As it happened, the sop to republican France merely provided respite from a war which began again in 1803 and and continued until the grand finale at Waterloo in 1815. During the interval, before the victory at Trafalgar on 21 October 1805, the giant shadow of Napoleon loomed ever larger over the English Channel, blotting out the orderly balances in Whitehall's ledgers. Nominally a possession of Holland, the Cape had become essentially a French protectorate, which France could exploit as a base for commerce raiders, and, conceivably, as a marshalling yard for an attack on India. Such a prospect was not beyond reason. By the middle of 1805 reports of an armament to be assembled at the Cape were too numerous to be ignored.

Yet in weighing the evidence, the Admiralty were bound to question the French objective. Were the apparent preparations designed as a feint to divert British forces from home waters? In the light of subsequent French manoeuvres, such a design seems highly probable; but in the end the government preferred not to risk the safety of their main road to India. In August 1805—some seven weeks *before* the battle of Trafalgar—an expedition, which included four ships-of-the-line and fifty-five transports containing more than 6,000 troops, set sail for Table Bay. On 6 January 1805 a landing was made without difficulty, and three days later the Dutch forces capitulated.

From the reconquered Cape northeastward to India, five islands played a part as strategic or simply as refreshment bases in helping to bridge the maritime gap—Portuguese Moçambique, Madagascar, the huge land of the Hovas and the Sakalava, Johanna, one of a group called collectively the Comoro Islands, Mauritius, known in the days of French possession as Ile de France, and Ceylon. In addition, there were some 500 smaller stepping stones, more or less on the route to Bombay, but few of them had good harbours. Some were inhabited and cultivated;

others were used as occasional fishing stations; the majority were little more than coral islets, completely submerged during the hurricane season and therefore highly dangerous to shipping.

Moçambique is a coral island about a mile and a half in length and a quarter mile in greatest breadth, sheltered by the mainland some five miles distant. Low-lying and sandy, with little vegetation apart from a few miserable palm trees, it was completely dependent for provisions on the adjacent coast. Indeed, Moçambique could only be regarded as an emergency refreshment port, whence a few pigs, goats, or poultry were procurable in time of dire need. In his narrative of the famous survey expedition in the 1820s Captain W. F. W. Owen (who, after his retirement in 1835, continued his surveys on Nova Scotian and Bay of Fundy coasts) has provided a melancholy picture of this Portuguese outpost with a background of squalor, decay, and death. That a handful of European inhabitants should have been able to endure for so long the corrosive effects of climate, disease, and political corruption was beyond his comprehension.[24]

Across the Moçambique Channel, the giant island of Madagascar stands directly athwart the main thoroughfare to India. Apart from a few missionaries and traders it had remained strangely aloof from the main tides of European imperialism that had swept fleets and armies to India and Ceylon. Over a period of a hundred and fifty years and more, European settlement had barely penetrated the forested lowlands behind the shoreline. Almost a thousand miles in length and averaging 250 miles in breadth, it possesses a curiously regular coastline. Along two-thirds of the eastern side, the shore runs very nearly in a straight

24. *Narrative of Voyages to explore the shores of Africa, Arabia, and Madagascar; performed in H.M. Ships, Leven and Barracouta*, 2 vols. (London, 1833), I, 190.

line, occasionally interrupted by stabbing reefs and by shifting sandbanks which block the mouths of small rivers, creating swamps and stagnant lagoons that once bred the notorious Madagascar fever. Not until the mid-eighteenth century did France have a firm foothold on the east coast. In 1750 French traders settled for a few years on the island of Ste. Marie on the northeast shore, and a little later at Foule Pointe, a few miles below. But prospects of a healthier existence tempted the surviving merchants to migrate further southward to Tamatave on the east coast.

Standing precariously on a spit of low-lying sandy soil about a mile long east and west, and half a mile broad, Tamatave had no protection against invading seas except a semicircular barrier of coral reefs. Yet this exposed and dangerous anchorage was the most important port in Madagascar. Tamatave fronts on the main street to India— the Outer Channel, and, more important, it directly faces Mauritius and Reunion, with which a flourishing bullock trade had been carried on for years. Yet when a British force occupied Tamatave in May 1811 they found fewer than forty French inhabitants; these included an officer and a few soldiers who were still working on the fortifications that Napoleon had ordered. France reoccupied Tamatave in 1816, but it could never become a naval base. Not until 1885 did she acquire, on the northern tip of Madagascar, not only the best harbour on the Island, but the most commanding site on the route between the Cape and Bombay. Diego-Suarez was to become before the end of the century the French alternative to the lost Ile de France.

About 180 miles to the northwest of Madagascar, on the direct route through the Inner Passage, the Comoro Islands—Comoro, Johanna, Mayotta, and Mohilla—were regarded by cruiser and Indiamen alike as emergency refreshment stations. Luxurious in their hill and mountain vegetation, they were ideal resorts for bored and scurvy-ridden crews in need of fresh meat, vegetables, and fruit;

but they lacked safe anchorages, and were inhabited by suspicious and often hostile natives. Johanna, a wedge-shaped island some 26 miles long, was the most frequented of the group, but the main harbour on the north side was only safe during the period of the southwest monsoon. For the rest of the year it was, like Table Bay at the Cape, open to the heavy surf that lashed the shoreline behind the ill-protected anchorage. Moreover, on an island so frequently ravaged by native invaders from Madagascar, it was impossible to tell from week to week whether or not the political situation would be conducive to friendly barter or surprise attack.

In time of European war, however, French men-of-war were far more dangerous than truculent Sakalava chieftains from Madagascar, and from their forbidding island base on the direct Cape to Bombay route, they threatened to hamstring the British trade connection with the East. This base, Ile de France, was, without rhetorical exaggeration, *the* key to French power in the Indian Ocean. Although the Portuguese had visited the island at the beginning of the sixteenth century they made no settlement. At the end of the sixteenth century, the Dutch took possession, and named it Mauritius after their Stadholder, Prince Maurice of Nassau. They abandoned it in 1710, and five years later they were succeeded by the French. Although the British East India Company had cast jealous eyes upon a rendezvous so neatly placed athwart the route to India, they could do little but urge its conquest, and their pleas were in vain. Meanwhile, the renamed Ile de France became the main French naval base and arsenal for the campaigns in India during the Austrian Succession and the Seven Years' wars, as well as the haunt of privateers who played havoc with Company commerce.

One overpowering reason why Ile de France was not an object of assault was its supposed impregnability. Under the energetic and imaginative Comte de La Bourdonnais, who was governor between 1735 and 1746, forts were built, troops poured in, and ordinary citizens enrolled in the militia. "The Island of Mauritius," wrote the chairman of the East India Company's Secret Committee to the secretary of state in August 1781, "is viewed by their Ministry in the same light as ours do Gibraltar; as this is the key to the Mediterranean, the French consider Mauritius the key to the Indian Ocean, and are in consequence determined to render it impregnable."[25]

Five hundred and fifty miles east of Madagascar and about 2,300 miles from the Cape of Good Hope, Mauritius rises behind the encircling ring of coral reefs like a huge triangular flatiron, some 36 miles long and about 23 miles broad at the base.[26] Port Louis, on the northwest coast, provided a small but snug harbour, well protected by barrier reefs, and therefore easily defensible from the sea. Port Bourbon possessed an anchorage almost equally secure, but since it was situated on the windward side of the island, ships found it difficult to beat their way out to sea.[27] Approaching the island at daybreak, even the sophisticated tourist is likely to be moved by the distant splendour of volcanic mountains rising like castle turrets in the misty morning air. A hundred and sixty years ago, however, British naval officers sent to spy out the inhospitable coast were more impressed by the navigational dangers.

25. Quoted in Richmond, *Navy in India*, p. 122.

26. Some 130 miles southwest of Mauritius and about 400 miles to the east of Madagascar, lies the island of Réunion, a mountainous lump, about a hundred miles in circumference, hemmed by coral reefs and intersected by two vast ravines which cross each other at right angles. Bourbon, as it was then called, was a vital auxiliary in the defences of Mauritius, but no more. It had no harbour worthy of the name, and only one place where ships could anchor in reasonable comfort; *Spencer Papers*, IV, 242.

27. Vice-Admiral Curtis to Spencer, 28 November 1800; *Spencer Papers*, IV, 242.

Access to the main harbour of Port St. Louis by narrow, twisted channels was difficult for French pilots in any weather; elsewhere even smugglers looked askance at the rock-bound coast, against which the surf beat unceasingly.

The dependence of Ile de France on outside sources of supply had been noted by Admiral Hughes during the War of American Independence, and attention had been called to the possibility of starving it into submission. Obviously a fortress island unable from its own resources to feed its defenders could not fulfil its function as a naval base. It might withstand a sudden assault but it could scarcely resist a prolonged blockade and siege. In 1794 an expedition had been discussed but nothing came of it. Again, five years after the capture of the Cape in 1795, the Governor-General of Bengal, Lord Mornington, told the commander-in-chief of the Cape squadron, Vice-Admiral Sir Roger Curtis, that he proposed to send an assault force from India early in 1801.[28] However real the prospect, the armistice of Amiens intervened, and not until after Trafalgar was further consideration given to the plan. In 1808, Curtis's successor at the Cape, Vice-Admiral Sir Albemarle Bertie, used every vessel he could spare from his reinforced squadron to starve out the Island, but a dozen sloops and frigates were insufficient to stop the many loopholes which allowed supplies to trickle through the reefs from Moçambique and Madagascar.

The reluctance of the Admiralty to support a full-dress attack was admittedly influenced by distractions in other theatres. But fear of the unknown was an equally impressive argument favouring delay. For more than half a century, stories of hurricanes and encircling barrier reefs had built up the legend of the impregnable Isle. Even if safe passage were found for the assault boats, where could one find a

28. 24 October 1800; *Spencer Papers*, IV, 159.

secure anchorage for the transports? Indeed, long after the conquest the jagged coral walls of Mauritius were regarded by the British garrison as the Island's chief defence.

Not until the end of 1809 was the decision taken to assault Ile de France, but further delays occurred, chiefly because of the difficulty of assembling a force combining squadrons from both the Cape and India. Not until the end of December 1810 did a British fleet of some seventy sail bear up for the point of debarkation on the north coast. Once a passage through the surf had been marked by buoys it was possible for the ships to move safely to an anchorage about three-quarters of a mile from shore, close to leeward of Cape Malheureux. No enemy opposition was encountered; not a shot was fired. Nonetheless, considering the difficulties of carrying men, artillery, ammunition, and stores through sinuous channels between coral reefs, the operation may be regarded as a minor triumph in the annals of assault landings. Four days later, after sporadic fighting, Ile de France capitulated, and the main threat to British security in the Indian Ocean was dissolved.[29] By the Treaty of Paris, 30 May 1814, "the scourge of British commerce" became a British possession; the nearest neighbour, the island of Bourbon, was handed back to France for the simple reason that, lacking a decent harbour, it was of no use.

Unless the need for refreshment or repairs forced a stop-over in the Seychelles, there were normally no breaks in the sailing track that led onwards to the west coast of India and Bombay. Bombay had always been the most valuable base in India—the only one with a dockyard—

29. The total British force, seamen and marines, numbered about 12,000 men. The French force, including militia, was scarcely 4,000; the professional garrison less than 1,600. A brief account is contained in G. S. Graham, *Great Britain in the Indian Ocean 1810–1850* (London, 1967), p. 51.

and between October and December, it was the only safe harbour on the entire mainland. The northeast monsoon, beginning with violent gales about mid-October, put shipping in the open roadsteads of the east coast in constant peril until January. The widely chronicled hurricane which swept British warships to disaster in 1749 had shown the fearful risks of wintering off Madras Roads. Hence, Admiralty instructions were specific, and became a rule. To avoid the northeast monsoon, ships were ordered to leave the Coromandel coast for Bombay before the end of the first week in October.

But recourse to Bombay during the height of the monsoon season meant that the Bay of Bengal was left undefended against any enemy force which might appear before the squadron had time to return to the Coromandel coast. La Bourdonnais had taken advantage of this fact during the War of the Austrian Succession. Thenceforward, successive engagements were fought in the off-shore waters between Madras and the southern promontory of Ceylon. The first general action between the squadrons of Pocock and d'Aché took place near Pondicherry in April 1758, when the Royal Navy gained command of the Bay of Bengal. During the War of the American Revolution, Suffren fought Hughes to a draw in five fierce battles off the Coromandel coast and Ceylon—a highly creditable French performance which, however, did little more than confirm the fact that the west coast of India, containing the principal harbour and dockyard of Bombay, was no longer, as in the seventeenth century, adjacent to a main theatre of conflict. The strategic centre of gravity had shifted to the Bay of Bengal, where not one harbour existed south of the tortuous channels which led to the unpopular Calcutta base far up the Hooghli River.

In other words, no continental Indian port could provide shelter throughout the year. Only by securing a base on the island of Ceylon, as Hughes had recognized, would it be possible to circumvent the seasonal monsoons. Given a sufficiently safe and commodious harbour, preferably on the east coast, ships could resume station once the violence of the monsoon had passed, and be in a position to take the offensive on the hitherto vulnerable Coromandel coast.

Separated from the southeast extremity of this coast by a narrow and shallow strait, Ceylon bears somewhat the same relationship to India as does Sicily to Italy. Approached from the west by ship, this last of the "luxury islands" is still a sight of moving beauty. The western coastline is low and fringed with coconut palms that grow to the very edge of the ocean and appear to be growing out of it. In the background, the fabled Adam's Peak rises like an eroded pyramid in the jungle—on clear days a welcome landmark for the most experienced navigator. But in the eighteenth century, few captains would willingly remain on the west coast beyond April unless specifically ordered. There were too many sandbanks and shoals, particularly to the northwest. The roadstead at Colombo was useful only between late September and early May; once the southwest monsoon set in, the harbour was open to violent winds and waves, not to speak of capricious and powerful currents.[30]

Despite an intimidating shoreline of rocky precipices, the east coast had always been more attractive to the sailing ships of those days. Apart from a few dangerous reefs, most of which had been marked, the coastal waters of the east coast were safer, better understood, and far simpler to navigate than those on the west. Moreover, near the northeast extremity, only 320 miles from Madras, the best harbour in the Indian Ocean awaited the attentions of the Admiralty's artificers.

Nelson had called Trincomalee the finest harbour in the world, and even today in semi-decay, it remains one of the

---

30. *West Coast of India Pilot*, 9th ed. (London, 1950), p. 107.

most magnificent—a huge crystal pool dotted with ornamental islands, enclosed by thick jungle, that once again is beginning to creep down to the edge of the shoreline. Tucked away in the corner of Kottiar Bay, the inner harbour, enclosed by rocky headlands and islands, covers an area of about twelve square miles. For generations the entrance was unmarked by a lighthouse. Nonetheless, to the knowledgeable pilot it was easily approachable and once inside, almost invulnerable.

Although a Dutch possession for the greater part of the eighteenth century, since 1746 Trincomalee had been regularly used by the Royal Navy as a refitting base. During the Seven Years' War the Dutch had remained neutral and friendly, and by 1762 the British had their own heaving-down wharf, repair shops, and facilities for obtaining wood and water. During the War of American Independence, following the entrance of the Netherlands into the war on the side of France, Trincomalee fell to a British force in January 1782, was recaptured by the French in August, and restored to the Dutch by the Treaty of Versailles in 1783. Meanwhile, the Royal Navy continued to make use of its facilities until Holland was overrun by the armies of Revolutionary France, and once again Britain was compelled to occupy unfriendly overseas ports in the interests of her Indian empire. When a short-lived peace was ratified by the Treaty of Amiens in March 1802, the Cape, as we have noticed, was returned to the Dutch, but Ceylon was kept.

Although the Admiralty never forgot that Trincomalee could command both coasts of India, "the finest harbour in the world" did not develop into a great naval base. For a moment in 1816, what was little more than an impoverished-looking repair and stores rendezvous came to life when the entire Madras establishment was ordered to be removed to Ceylon. But the momentum generated by Admiralty impulsiveness faded under the pressures for economy and retrenchment that followed Waterloo. The British government was still nervous about the future security of India, yet sufficiently confident of the advantages of cutting expenses to pay off thousands of seamen, and reduce the East Indies squadron to a fraction of its war-time strength—two or three fourth-rates or frigates and four or five sloops.[31] In February 1822 it was decided that the still uncompleted base should be allowed to run down, with the gradual withdrawal of personnel and the abandonment of hospital, repair shops, victualling reserves, and naval stores. Bases like squadrons were, except in times of crisis, at the mercy of Treasury accountants, and Trincomalee was but an extreme example of nineteenth-century parsimony in practice. The Cape and Gibraltar were also victims of the 1822 purge; the remaining overseas yards, including the Canadas, received the axe in 1826.

Meanwhile, Bombay with its dockyard became what in reality it had always been in peacetime, the main rendezvous of the squadron; Trincomalee barely survived as a port for refreshment, minor repairs, and limited stores. By 1832 it had neither a resident naval commissioner, a purser, a surgeon, nor a carpenter; the only official of consequence provided by the Admiralty was a boatswain.[32] When the acquisition of Hong Kong in 1842 gave the Navy an important harbour off a commercially rich coastline, the Admiralty ordered further reductions in Ceylon. By 1845 more men were employed at the Hong Kong base than at Trincomalee. Although officially designated as the main victualling depot for the Indian Ocean division of the East Indies squadron, its day was done. Not for another hundred years did it resume a vigorous existence. Early in 1942 the Japanese captured Singapore, bombed Darwin, and completed the occupation of Hong Kong. The

31. Graham, *Great Britain in the Indian Ocean*, p. 319.
32. Ibid., p. 327.

immediate consequence was Trincomalee's return to action. Docks and yards were repaired, the Admiral's house redecorated, and for a brief interval the obdurate jungle was forced back from the "magnificent lake" which once possessed the key to India.

In conclusion, one may pose the question: Did economic factors seriously or positively affect the choice of any of Britain's eastern naval bases? In the case of the Cape the answer is quite clear. Although there were positive military advantages, particularly during war, in having one or more staging posts to India, the Cape was never regarded as an object of territorial conquest. It was expected to be, and for many years proved to be, an economic liability.[33] British projects to capture the Cape, first in 1781, then in 1795, and finally in 1805, were directly and solely concerned with keeping this strategic pivot of two oceans out of the hands of the French. Even after the garrison had been reduced to a skeleton establishment, expenditure on defence in the thirties was never less than £100,000 a year, and during successive Kaffir wars was more than doubled.[34]

As for Mauritius, like the Cape it was taken in order to deprive the French of a useful and potentially dangerous base on the route to India. Here again, the economic temptations were non-existent. The Island had been settled for generations and in the most productive areas, close to the coast, sugar cane had taken root and become the principal staple. Yet Mauritius was far from self-sufficient, depending heavily on outside sources for its food supply. A good deal of rice and most of the cattle

33. Of the exports from the colony after 1815, only two commodities, wine and wool, were of any importance, and it was a long time before even wool counted significantly in competition with other producing areas of the world.

34. John S. Galbraith, *Reluctant Empire, British Policy on the South African Frontier, 1834–54* (Cambridge, 1965), p. 36.

came from Madagascar. In normal times the Cape sent corn and various other provisions, but most of the grain came from the neighbouring and more fertile island of Bourbon. Actually there was good farming land in the interior bordering on the timber forests, and efforts had been directed from Paris to increase cultivation by means of slave labour. But in time of war, any significant expansion of agriculture was always counter-balanced by increasing numbers of hungry mouths, represented by reinforcements of solders and seamen.

Trincomalee might have suffered less had it subsequently revealed, like Singapore (whose docking facilities were nonetheless neglected until the outbreak of World War I),[35] some special capacity as an entrepôt. Unfortunately, commercial shipping made little use of the harbour, which was three hundred miles off the developing steam route to China. Even at the height of the monsoon season, paddle-wheelers with the improved compound engines of the late thirties, had less need than the sailing ship to seek shelter and succour in the best-protected harbour in the East. Moreover, the hinterland remained unexploited apart from the scanty efforts of native labourers who were suspected of being plague carriers.[36]

In brief, particular business or general commercial interests counted for little or nothing in the negotiations which led to the acquisition of the Cape, Mauritius or Trincomalee, and, one might add, Aden. The security and prosperity of an already vast British Empire, Castlereagh took pains to explain to the prime minister, Lord Liver-

---

35. Graham, *Politics of Naval Supremacy*, p. 53 n.

36. The encircling jungle did contain innumerable ponds of stagnant water, and cholera did smite Trincomalee with unhappy regularity. But fevers and plagues were not responsible for the failure. The same epidemics were just as common in India, and in every other Asian port. On the whole, Trincomalee was no worse and probably a good deal healthier than any other naval base in the Indian Ocean.

pool, in 1814, depended not on the acquisition of potentially embarrassing and expensive plantations, but on a well-distributed network of ports and bases.[37] Strategic bases were vital to the protection of Britain's overseas communications; they allowed the Royal Navy sufficient mobility to secure the trading lines that brought life to the central organism, the British Isles.

Economic considerations did indeed work negatively, as in the case of Cape Colony in 1802, discouraging a permanent occupation. But they never positively influenced the choice of a naval base. Such a choice was much more likely to be affected by geography and the state of international politics than by the prospect of economic gain. Certainly, in so far as this study is concerned, the supreme economic interest lay not with the base, whatever kind of colonial establishment it might warrant. It lay simply in the extent to which that base helped to safeguard the vital sea route to India.

37. See letter of 19 April 1814; Harlow and Madden, *British Colonial Developments 1774–1834, Select Documents* (Oxford, 1953), pp. 14–15; also C. K. Webster, *The Foreign Policy of Castlereagh, 1812–1815* (London, 1931), pp. 272–3, 491, and G. S. Graham, *Empire of the North Atlantic*, 2nd ed. (London, 1958), pp. 262–4.

4 PAX BRITANNICA AND THE BALANCE OF POWER IN THE NINETEENTH CENTURY

In the nineteenth century, by achieving what it is still proper to call "command of the sea", Britain was able to exercise an international power far out of proportion to her resources and population. With island bases and mainland trading stations in every sea, a world-wide British empire was held together commercially and strategically by communication routes extending from the English Channel and the home ports of the United Kingdom. Only a powerful fleet was capable of severing these overseas connections, and during the nineteenth century no attempt was made to do this. No European nation possessed the means to transport safely and in quantity the arms and the men sufficient to challenge Britain's imperial hegemony. However indeterminate its effects on self-sufficient countries of the continent, sea power could be decisive in its effects overseas.

Britain's preponderant influence in the world reached its peak at a time when all the great powers were European states. It was the period when the expression "European states system" was nearly synonymous with international politics. It was also a period when overland transport was everywhere slow and costly. For West European countries, communication by way of the Atlantic ocean and connecting seas was nearly as important as for insular Britain. The bulk of their maritime traffic had to pass through one or more constricting seaways—the Channel, the North Sea, the Strait of Gibraltar, and (after 1869) the Suez Canal and the Red Sea. By occupying shore positions near those focal sea areas, and by maintaining token forces in the vicinity, British statesmen kept their European adversaries constantly reminded of the Royal Navy's ability to deny them access.[1] Until nearly the end of the nineteenth century, the ability to control the narrow sea corridors leading to and from Europe insured against competition the integrity and safety of the British Empire. "Five keys lock up the world!" wrote Admiral Sir John Fisher in 1904, "Singapore, the Cape, Alexandria, Gibraltar, Dover. These five keys belong to England."[2]

There was little or no military advantage in territorial occupation overseas, and almost certainly considerable financial loss. Like the Whig businessmen of Anne's reign, the new generation of industrial go-getters born in the factory age were chiefly concerned not with acquiring

1. H. and M. Sprout, "The Dilemma of Rising Demands and Insufficient Resources," in *World Politics*, XX, no. 4 (July 1968), 666.

2. Quoted, A. J. Marder, *The Anatomy of British Sea Power* (New York, 1940), p. 473; H. and M. Sprout, "Dilemma of Rising Demands," 667.

colonies but with gaining access to new sources of supply, as well as new markets. Of course, such ambitions had territorial implications; the conquest of an island or political domination over a particular strategic area could mean protection against the military threat or the trade competition of a rival.

But this form of expansion was accomplished without the financial burden of a large military establishment on land. Like Singapore, which was acquired in 1819, or Hong Kong in 1842, all or nearly all of these colonies or bases were situated close to salt water, either upon an island or at the end of a peninsula, or like Aden (1839) on a defensible natural harbour backed by mountains. Since these overseas bases rarely offered unprotected flanks or rears, relatively small garrisons, sometimes composed of volunteers, sufficed to man the principal forts and strong points.

British sea power could never guarantee their continuous security; the Royal Navy could not at any given moment count on commanding all maritime communications and focal areas. Nations do not ordinarily expect to have to fight the rest of the world, and no nation in history has ever made budgetary provision for such a contingency. The measure of British naval strength in the nineteenth century was, allowing for episodic panics, determined by the strength of prospective adversaries. Generally speaking, so long as her superiority over at least two of her real or potential rivals was not threatened, Britain had no reason to spend heavily on warships. During the first half of the nineteenth century, budget estimates were reduced by more than a half, and the effective strength of the fleet was correspondingly reduced.[3] In 1814, 99 ships-of-the-line were in commission; by 1838 only 22.

---

3. G. S. Graham, *Empire of the North Atlantic*, 2nd ed. (Toronto, 1958), p. 266; C. J. Bartlett, *Great Britain and Sea Power 1815–1854* (Oxford, 1963), pp. 13–29, 59–65.

Since British predominance on the oceans was virtually unassailable, foreign competition for colonies overseas rarely affected Britain's relations with Europe until nearly the last two decades of the century. But this acceptance of maritime supremacy did not include the Mediterranean, wherein Britain by reason of geography was regarded as an intruder. As the Indian Empire grew in majesty and commercial importance, Britain was increasingly concerned about the safety of this landlocked corridor on the way to India. Indeed, its security became fundamental to her foreign policy. If need be, she was prepared to keep that route open by force of arms. During the Napoleonic wars France had threatened India by striking at British communications with the East. Memories of Napoleonic intervention in Egypt lingered, and fears of renewed adventures were revived in 1830, when Charles X bridged the Mediterranean by establishing a colonial beachhead in Algeria. It could be assumed that this was the first stage in an avenging process aimed at severing the Overland-Red Sea route to India.

Unless one admits the measure in which tradition affects national moods and governs national policies, it is difficult to explain early British fears of convalescent France. As in the days of the elder Pitt, France seemed destined to remain the hereditary enemy. In retrospect, the reluctance to recognize Russia as principal foe and imperial rival is hard to comprehend. Of all the great powers, Britain and Russia alone faced each other in areas beyond the European heartland. After 1815 Russia was in a far stronger position than France to exert pressure on Britain's Overland route to India. Because Russia possessed a strong Black Sea fleet, she could (as was demonstrated in 1833 when a Russian squadron arrived at Constantinople) exert enormous leverage on the Straits which, once unlocked, opened the way to the eastern Mediterranean and the vital isthmus of Suez. To ensure that Russian ships stayed within the Black Sea, Britain eventually recognized the need to bolster Turkey as a protective buffer. The Turkish Empire in Asia, pivoting on Constantinople, remained India's first line of defence against Russian aggression throughout most of the nineteenth century.

Not until the 1840s did British fears of Russian ambitions extend beyond the Straits. By that time, British statesmen were beginning to have spasmodic nightmares (which the Crimean War did not exorcize), as they contemplated the Russian bear shambling down the Euphrates Valley and settling permanently beside the Persian Gulf. If Russia, it was argued, could establish a fortified port near the mouth of the Tigris-Euphrates, she might win control of the Gulf and be in a position to outflank all the main routes leading to the East. The mere threat of such action would involve a reorganization of British naval resources in Indian ocean waters where command had hitherto been safely preserved by a couple of frigates and a dozen or so sloops.

It is extremely unlikely that any Russian government considered such an operation, or was ever seriously attracted by dreams of Indian conquest. Had Russian troops reached the Gulf, any effort at establishing a base would have been neutralized by the Royal Navy. Even had a decent harbour been available on that desolate coast, Russian command of the Gulf was simply out of the question. The honourable gentlemen in Whitehall and Downing Street, remarked Joseph Hume with sardonic relish, "had talked so much about Russia, that they were afraid of a monster they had created."[4]

The master key to India's security lay not in the Persian Gulf but in the Straits, where the empire of the Ottomans blocked Russian access to the Bosphorus. Yet that recumbent hulk could easily disintegrate. Successive treaties

4. Debate of 4 March 1836; Committee of Supply–Naval Estimates (*Hansard*, 3rd ser., XXXI, 1235–6).

intended to bolster the Sublime Porte offered no surety that Turkish dominions could be maintained intact. The Sultan's feudatory, Mehemet Ali—the real ruler of Egypt —was no more capable of guaranteeing passage to the Red Sea than the Sultan himself. Moreover, against a possible alliance of European powers, such as had occurred during the War of American Independence, Britain was incapable, single-handed, of sustaining Turkey and holding open the Overland route. The haunting and not improbable spectre that confronted ministers in Downing Street was of a Britain standing alone, in perilous isolation.[5]

Supposing France and Russia came together in unholy partnership—France to get Egypt and possibly Syria, and Russia to occupy Constantinople and conceivably establish authority in Persia whose policies she was already shaping? Such a prospect fostered the true British nightmare—a Continental alliance from which she was excluded.

The British government and the Admiralty were acutely aware of their inability to cope with a sudden onslaught. In the event, say, of a Franco-British crisis, France might well strike without notice, and seize the Isthmus long before reinforcements, naval and military, could reach Alexandria. Britain might retain her all-round supremacy at sea, but she had not sufficient ships to safeguard continuously the inland corridor to India.[6] During the early months of the Near East crisis in 1839, the French possessed numerically superior forces in the Mediterranean, and at one moment Palmerston seriously considered calling in "ten Russian sail of the line."[7] Had Russia joined with

5. See G. S. Graham, *The Politics of Naval Supremacy* (Cambridge, 1965), pp. 70–72.

6. In 1838 the Royal Navy possessed 22 ships-of-the-line, of which 9 were in the Mediterranean at the beginning of the year. By 1839 the total had risen to nearly 30, of which 11, by July, were stationed in the Mediterranean (*Navy List, 1836–9*).

7. Bartlett, *Great Britain and Sea Power*, p. 132.

France, Britain would, in the language of Disraeli, have been "dished."

To avoid such a catastrophe, the obvious aim of British foreign policy was to isolate one rival power by courting the other, and this British statesmen, with the considerable aid of Providence, were fortunate in accomplishing. In 1840 Britain, Austria, Prussia, and Russia blocked French efforts to support Mehemet Ali of Egypt against the Sultan. Following this rebuff of France, the balance of power had to be readjusted a few years later to meet the challenge of Russia. In 1854–5 during the Crimean War, France and Britain joined forces to safeguard the independence of Turkey; and again, in 1878, following Russian penetration of the Balkans, Britain sought agreement with Austria, and sent a squadron to defend Constantinople.

British diplomacy was activated by what had become standard doctrine: the maintenance of the *status quo* in the Near East. Throughout the Eastern Crisis of 1876–8, Gladstone, in opposition, had condemned any suggestion that Britain should take over Egypt, as stoutly as Palmerston, from the forties to the sixties, had opposed the construction of a French canal across the isthmus of Suez. When Ferdinand de Lesseps' canal was finally opened in 1869, it was controlled, theoretically at least, by an international corporation. The rejection by the Disraeli ministry (1874–80) of Bismarck's sly hints that Egypt might be acquired by a *coup de main* was in keeping with orthodox policy, namely, that of avoiding any drastic intervention that might disturb the uneasy European balance of power. Britain still aimed at keeping the Ottoman Empire intact as a means of preventing France or Russia from muscling in.

The upset of British plans and past hopes came in July 1882 when Admiral Seymour shelled the fortifications of Alexandria in an effort to safeguard European interests and Turkish suzerainty in Egypt against the mounting violence of Colonel Ahmed Arabi's nationalists. Fearful of Bismarckian intrigue behind the scenes, France, hitherto fully cooperative, refused to share an operation of war that might mean a costly drain on her European resources. When an invitation to Italy was similarly rejected, Britain was left to restore order alone. In consequence, she found herself in sole occupation of the country.

Although Gladstone had sought the approval of other powers in 1882 (only Germany supported and encouraged British involvement), he was not trying to whitewash an intervention which he resented, regretted, and swore to be only temporary. Nonetheless, his action broke a unique interlude in modern European history. Up until the occupation of Egypt, Britain counted on her capacity as a non-aligned arbitrator to gather allies in support of a stable Europe. She was the one power that consistently opposed change; she was willing to support Turkey, Greece, or Egypt against any aggressor who seemed likely to disturb the European balance. By occupying Egypt, she upset a precarious equilibrium which for more than half a century she had done her best to preserve in the interests of home and imperial security. The result was twenty years of conflict with France, and the dismal prospect, which became grim reality by the end of the century, of isolation.[8]

Up to that point, how important was the Royal Navy in helping to preserve the vital status quo, which within the world context has been called the Pax Britannica? The primary object of British policy, as we have noted, was to find the essential allied support on the Continent. To what extent did the post-1815 navy add force to the diplomatic

8. See in this connection, K. H. W. Hilborn, "British Policy and Diplomacy in the Near East during the Liberal Administrations, August 1892–June 1895" (Ph.D. diss., Oxford University, 1960).

lever? Or to vary the metaphor, did command of the sea in the age of laissez-faire count as heavily in the scales of the European balance as it did during the eighteenth century?

Certainly, during the first forty years or so after Waterloo the prestige of the navy within Britain remained low and its development as a fighting service was severely circumscribed financially—conditions which have often led to the assumption that the power factor could be ignored in the age of Pax Britannica. In the beginning, the constant clamours for economy struck angry sparks from some of the old admirals, who had retained from the Napoleonic wars an inbred consciousness of the meaning of sea power in relation to empire. But after they had passed away, there were few in parliament, or in the country generally, to preserve the tradition and teach the lessons of experience. There was "scarcely an officer now fit for service," wrote Vice-Admiral Sir William Bowles in 1852, "who has ever commanded a squadron at sea, and the whole of our rising generation are (without any fault of their own) perfectly inexperienced in the manoeuvres of a fleet!"[9]

There was substance in the nostalgic rhetoric of Blackwood's *Edinburgh Magazine*: "We see a navy, once the terror and glory of the world, silently melting away under the wish to buy good articles cheap; and our army, which once struck down Napoleon, suffered to dwindle into insignificance lest its numbers should excite the discontent of the tradesmen in our manufacturing towns!"[10] "If certain economists have their way," said the *Quarterly Review* in 1830, "although history may record our glories in war, she will describe us as having sunk into a nation of petti-fogging shop-keepers during the period of peace

9. *Thoughts on National Defence*, 3rd ed. (London, 1852), p. xii.
10. XXXIX (1836), 792.

which followed these exertions."[11] Until Palmerston began to cry panic during the debates of 1844–5, and until the Duke of Wellington initiated his own naval scare of 1847 with the pronouncement that steam had bridged the English Channel, the state of the Royal Navy was not a vital parliamentary issue.

Almost inevitably then, the period of the thirties and early forties witnessed continuous reductions of the Royal Navy. Reconciled to being the principal object of government economies, and already confused by technological revolutions, which were shortly to make the old line-of-battle ships obsolete, even the Admiralty bowed before the slogans of the economists. Commerce, not ships, they were told, was the safeguard of peace, and therefore of national security.

Between 1815 and 1840 naval estimates were reduced by almost half. In 1816 they were £9.5 million; in 1817 they went down to £6 million. Sir James Graham, the first Lord of the Admiralty, aimed to cut costs still further, and he succeeded in paring the total from £5.3 million in 1830 to £4.5 million in 1834.[12]

It was an incredibly small price to pay for nineteenth-century global supremacy. From the 1830s until the end of the century, the combined cost of army and navy in time of peace varied between two and three percent of the national income. At the peak of British power and influence, the decade of the 1860s, total expenditure for military purposes averaged less than £30 million a year.

Nonetheless, Britain did maintain her primacy on the oceans. But can one estimate with any confidence how much political leverage British diplomats derived from this fact? It has been suggested that the legend of British

11. XLII (1830), 520.
12. Six years later following the Near East crisis of 1839 naval estimates went up again to £5.5 million.

naval invincibility, firmly rooted in historic achievement, exerted a strong psychological influence on Britain's rivals as well as on British statesmen themselves. Throughout nearly a century of comparative peace and dwindling defence budgets, decisive battles like Trafalgar were not forgotten, and the presence of the Royal Navy (often only a nominal presence) in distant ports and harbours of the world served to keep green the memories of past British naval prowess. Conceivably "showing the flag" in every sea fostered in the mind of the foreigner a presumption that Britain could again in an emergency close the main sea highways to her enemies.[13]

One cannot, unfortunately, assess the contribution of intangibles like prestige. On the other hand, it is clear that the achievement of what became known as the Pax Britannica was never the simple consequence of naval power, real or remembered. The navy was undoubtedly the indispensable prop of British diplomacy, but the safety of the Empire depended in the long run, as in the eighteenth century, on Britain's ability to enlist allied support on the continent of Europe.

This devotion to the policy of a European balance carried the inevitable risks associated throughout history with power politics. During the nineteenth century, however, it was favoured by unusual circumstances, the most significant of which was the disinclination of European powers to risk stability and prosperity in general war. Admittedly no economic motive is sufficient to explain what in retrospect appears as a European Indian summer. Yet it can be argued that this unique age of Pax Britannica was in part the result of Britain's phenomenal commercial development and consequent industrial supremacy. The fact that the great market of the United Kingdom together

13. H. and M. Sprout, "Dilemma of Rising Demands," 667–8.

with the wider markets of an enormous empire was steadily opening to the products of other states not only stimulated general economic activity, it contributed to relax international tensions within the whole trading world. If maritime power were unattainable for rival nations, this was not true of wealth; the commerce of the world was increasingly shared; inequalities of natural resources were alleviated by accessible Open Doors. In other words, the growth of free trade was introducing a kind of international equality in world commerce; the sharing of economic benefits, by discouraging envy, encouraged acquiescence in the British hegemony.

For the greater part of the nineteenth century, British ascendancy in the fields of industry, finance, commerce, and shipping was complete. No other power had sufficiently developed its industrial resources to offer serious competition. The iron, coal, and other basic materials required for military production were available within the British Isles, and British manpower was sufficient to exploit them. In terms of a war economy she was self-sufficient. The shift from timber to iron in ship construction, the introduction of armour plate and the shell-firing rifled gun gave an enormous advantage to the country possessing the most advanced metallurgical mills and capable of the largest production of pig iron.[14] Similarly, during the course of evolution from sail to steam, the possession of vast coalfields and well-distributed coaling stations confirmed the pre-eminence which had been acquired in two centuries of commercial and territorial expansion under sail.

Master of all she surveyed, Britain was therefore in a unique position to scrap traditional doctrines of national advantage, and to influence by example the trend towards

14. See William E. Livezey, "Sea Power in a Changing World," *Marine Corps Gazette* (U.S.A.), May 1949, pt. II.

free trade. Because her imperial security was rarely threatened after 1805 there was no need for any ostentatious assertion of maritime rights. Economic predominance was simply not compatible with military weakness; and because no jealous disputants were capable of seriously challenging her maritime supremacy, British policies of economic cooperation in terms of free trade, peace, and prosperity, were generally acceptable.[15]

It is true that British squadrons were used on occasion to effect specific ends whether in Greece, Latin America, or China, but it would be wrong to suggest that the Royal Navy imposed a British peace on the world. There was, for example, no effort to stop the French from entering Algiers in 1830 or Mexico in 1863 or Indo-China in the sixties, nor to keep the Americans out of Japan in the fifties or the North from blockading the South during the American Civil War. Britain was in no position either to seek or to ensure the peace of mankind by means of her fleet. "We cannot afford to be Knight Errant of the World," Lord Rosebery told Queen Victoria, "careering about to redress grievances and help the weak."[16]

On the other hand, the general quiescence of European powers gave Britain the opportunity to use her navy not only as a means of conducting anything from a demonstration to a local war, but as an effective restraining force which, on the whole, functioned in the interests of the European balance. The result was a kind of political stabilization which suggested to more optimistic Free Traders in the fifties and sixties the possibility of continuous material progress by the peaceful process of turning guns into ploughshares.

In short, although power was sacrificed during this

15. See Graham, *Politics of Naval Supremacy*, pp. 118–21.
16. The Marquess of Crewe, *Lord Rosebery*, 2 vols. (London, 1931), II, 426.

peaceful interlude, it was not surrendered. The leading exponent of progress through peace had not turned pacifist under the influence of free trade. The policy of sacrifice, if such it may be called, was one of defending the British empire at the least cost, and the expenses of imperial administration could most conveniently, profitably, and even safely, be reduced by cutting naval expenditure.

This could be done *safely* because, despite all the economies, the margin of security was far greater during the nineteenth century than at the beginning of the twentieth, when the rise of strong naval powers outside as well as in Europe began to threaten the British two-power standard. Despite the penny-pinching of Cabinets and the resulting reductions in armed strength, it was possible to maintain naval supremacy on the cheap. The sword of British naval power could still be an instrument of compulsion as well as prestige, although it was rarely withdrawn more than halfway from the scabbard. A preponderant weight of sea power was still concentrated in British hands, and its possession not only guaranteed the security of trade routes on the high seas, it provided an ever-ready instrument of diplomatic pressure that might be exercised, not necessarily silently, but with a minimum of international fuss and bloodshed.[17]

To maintain the Open Door in its fullest sense meant "power in evidence": the publicity value of the whiff of grapeshot was not despised. Even the pacific Lord Aberdeen saw the need for such "naval pomp and parade." "They have felt our power," he wrote in September 1844, "and they must continue to see that we are superior to other Nations if we mean to retain that ascendancy we have obtained in China."[18] This philosophy of persuasion was fully understood by the merchants of Britain. "The manu-

17. See Graham, *Politics of Naval Supremacy*, pp. 110–11.
18. Quoted in W. G. Beasley, *Great Britain and the Opening of Japan, 1834–58* (London, 1951), p. 58.

facturers of Yorkshire and Lancashire," exclaimed Richard Cobden in 1857, "look upon India and China as a field of enterprise which can only be kept open by force."[19]

There is, therefore, no need to over-idealize the motives which energized Free Trade Britain. Whatever the reductions in military expenditure, she did not really put in jeopardy the safety of her overseas communications; nor did she count on the philosophy of free trade as fully effective insulation against war. Other nations might enjoy the use of sea lanes and profit by the patrol work of British sloops and frigates. But in the event of an emergency, benevolent watch and ward was readily transmutable into positive domination.

Nonetheless, it must not be forgotten that British supervision of the oceans of the world, however velvet the glove, was possible only so long as other countries were willing to accept dependence on the philosophy and will of another state, and were not actively determined to reduce or eliminate the special advantages which that power derived from her naval supremacy. When the time came for European states to re-examine their national policies in the light of their prospective industrialization and when they started to enlarge and re-equip their own factories, build their own steam machinery, and weld their own iron hulls, the age of Pax Britannica had come to a close.

The delayed impact of this revolution has obscured its fundamental importance in history. Indeed, so pervasive was the myth of Pax Britannica that it diverted the attention of contemporaries from changes—economic and political—that from mid-century onward had begun gradually to erode the historic foundations of British supremacy. The crucial turning-point was reached almost a hundred years ago when European nations, suddenly

19. Quoted in William D. Grampp, *The Manchester School of Economics* (Stanford, 1960), p. 102.

aware that science had upset the balance between offence and defence in favour of the weaker power, initiated their own technological revolutions. Such developments were concerned not only with weapons, missiles, armour, tools, and tactics, but with the whole organization and control of what are called strategic materials. In the eighteenth century the power of a state had often been measured in terms of bullion, sugar, spices, masts, or timber. In the new age, the elements of military strength were to be found in raw materials such as coal, tin, copper, wool—and later on nickel, tungsten, cotton, oil, and rubber—many of which were only available in distant areas overseas.

Coerced by the depression of the seventies into abandoning free trade for protection, the major powers of Europe began to assume that a key to greater self-sufficiency and strength lay in actually controlling as much productive overseas territory as they could lay hands on. It was not British abuse of her naval supremacy, and of her almost monopolistic control of the oceans, that ultimately led other European nations to aggressive policies of overseas expansion and annexation. Such nations were guided by political considerations of prestige and impelled by their own economic growth.

In an age when the machines of industry had begun to erase the heavy premium that geography, ships, and seamanship had given to Great Britain, ambitious and well-endowed countries were offered new and tempting vistas of military capacity, influence, and independence.[20] Command of the sea was obviously beyond their reach; on the other hand, it might be pushed beyond the reach of the benevolent disposer whose White Ensign had for so long symbolized monopoly in three great oceans. Hence, without much understanding of how the ships were to be used, they proceeded compulsively, in the manner of

20. Graham, *Politics of Naval Supremacy*, p. 122.

Germany, to build navies to support national policies—policies that were a direct consequence of industrial and technological revolutions. In other words, the search for overseas resources with which to feed the new machinery of industrial revolutions helped to drive otherwise moderate governments into expensive military competition—a fantastic race whose course was marked by accumulations of triple-expansion engines and turbines, torpedo-boats and submarines, bigger guns and heavier armour.

Under the impact of these scientific and technological advances British command of the sea began to disintegrate, and by the end of the century the principle of universal command had to be surrendered in favour of a strategy of concentration in home waters. France, Russia, Turkey, Germany, and the United States were openly hostile; an uneasy balance of power had been succeeded by uncomfortable isolation. During the Venezuelan Crisis of 1895, following Britain's refusal to submit to American demands for an arbitrated settlement of the disputed boundary between British Guiana and Venezuela, Lord Salisbury found himself helpless against the stone wall of the Monroe Doctrine. Britain's narrow margin of superiority over the Austro-German Dual Alliance in European waters made impossible the reinforcement of the North American and West Indies squadron.

Six years later the Hay-Pauncefote treaty, providing for American rather than joint Anglo-American control of the proposed Panama Canal, signalized the surrender of the British position of equality in the Caribbean. No longer able to sustain command in the western Atlantic, Britain had taken the first step towards conciliating a non-European naval rival, the United States. The second step—the Japanese Alliance of 1902—was simply a confirmation of the fact that she could no longer distribute her naval forces over two hemispheres and maintain the cherished two-power standard in the face of an unfavourable European balance.

It is a curious but not unprecedented commentary on the work of influential thinkers that Admiral Mahan's exposition of the influence of sea power on the course of European and American expansion should have occurred at the very time when new instruments of war were beginning to erode the principles upon which his doctrines of command had been based. With the introduction of the submarine and the aeroplane, an empire based on control of maritime communications by surface ships was no longer possible.

On the other hand, Mahan's pronouncements had not, in the broadest sense, lost their validity. During two world wars the security of ocean routes was probably of greater significance than ever before in history. The safe transfer of strategic war materials, especially from North America, was vital to a favourable military balance, but that military balance was in turn contingent, as always, on a favourable political balance. In 1914–18, and again in 1939–45, British survival depended eventually on a maritime supremacy made possible by the North American alliance.

In the building of the British Empire, the surface ship was the vital instrument; but naval supremacy *per se* was never sufficient to ensure the safety of that many-storied edifice. The successful use of the Royal Navy as the adaptable tool of British diplomacy depended, in the nineteenth century, on the readiness of one or other European powers to cooperate with Britain in the interest of Continental stability. The task of British statesmen was to meet unanticipated crises or upsetting changes of alignment by successive adjustments of the balance. "Spendid isolation" was never the basis of British foreign policy except in so far as it meant a refusal to accept specific commitments. Until the 1880s—or, more precisely, until the occupation of Egypt—it was the maintenance of a diplomatic equilibrium in Europe that permitted a unique period of British maritime ascendancy—"the age of Pax Britannica."

5 RETREAT FROM EMPIRE
A Retrospect

Shortly before the end of the First World War, the village of Markham, Ontario, celebrated Empire Day in the local fair grounds. As a minor contributor to this patriotic festival, I stood on a makeshift platform and recited an uplifting piece of verse which I had fished out of a British weekly magazine called *The Boy Scout*. I can remember only the opening lines:

> Stand up for Britain, stand up today;
> Stand and salute the Union Jack.

How incongruous such a performance would appear today, when we are either exhilarated, blinded, or bored by the gaudy lights of nationalism, and sometimes shaken by its parochial manifestations. Yet fifty years ago my generation believed in the beneficence of an Empire for which so many Canadians had offered their lives. Many of us were brought up in a tradition which held that the "Old Country" was home, or at least a second home; and we found in the Royal Navy and the Indian Army, in Henty and Kipling, in Roberts and Kitchener, windows into other worlds as well as an inspiration that reinforced our commitment.

We waved Union Jacks when we sang of Empire fifty years ago, but we were romantics rather than jingoes. Few of us felt called upon to beat "the war-drum of the white-man." We sang "Rule Britannia," but not as colonial expatriates. The Empire was something a good deal bigger than Britain; it offered vistas of exotic life beyond the bounds of school and parish, province and nation. As a citizen of the British Empire one could, at least in imagination, rove the universe. "Her husband's to Aleppo gone," muttered the First Witch in *Macbeth*, "master o' the Tiger." The *Tiger* did sail to Aleppo—perhaps Shakespeare saw her weigh anchor—carrying two merchants who made their way through Persia and India as far as Malacca.[1]

The Empire offered careers not only for Christian missionaries, but for the spirited adventurer questing new horizons and old mysteries—the soldier, the botanist, the doctor, the miner, the farmer, the engineer, and the merchant. In retrospect, this yearning and this effort to breach the walls of parochial existence represented the first naïve steps towards a Western internationalism—a commitment to the beckoning outside world that was by no means always based on money-making.

Admittedly, there was something arrogant and vulgar about certain aspects of the imperial idea, and the notion of white superiority was taken for granted. On the other hand, we were not unprepared to combine our adolescent patriotism with sturdy faith in a God of Battles who would act as imperial umpire: God would judge the fruits of Empire in the years to come. He had come down on the

1. See A. L. Rowse, *The Expansion of Elizabethan England* (London, 1955), pp. 160, 197-8.

side of the righteous in 1918, and we had little foreboding about the future. No more than our fathers, did we stop to ponder Rudyard Kipling's early warning:

> Far-called, our navies melt away;
> On dune and headland sinks the fire:
> Lo, all our pomp of yesterday
> Is one with Nineveh and Tyre.

When Kipling wrote the "Recessional" in 1897 the Royal Navy was far less powerful than in 1918, but its relative superiority to other powers was considerably greater. The submarine was in its infancy and the airplane was still tied to earth. Pax Britannica had depended heavily in the nineteenth century on a European equilibrium, but even as late as 1918 the true state of the balance of power was veiled from west to east by the smoke of ten thousand new factory chimneys. Few in 1918 could have believed that both Germany and Japan were capable of forging new armaments of lethal violence that would within two decades place Empire and Commonwealth in peril. The United States was turning her immense strength in the direction of salt water, but to the less thoughtful onlooker Britain still seemed capable of retaining her traditional role of "mistress of the seas."

As I have tried to emphasize in a previous chapter, the most important element influencing Britain's superiority over any other power or most combinations of powers in the nineteenth century was her self-sufficiency in terms of essential war resources. For almost half a century before Kipling wrote his sombre appeal to the Almighty, British power had rested on the incomparable development of British industry. The coal, iron and steel, and other basic materials necessary for war production were available within Great Britain, and she possessed the skilled manpower to exploit them. No one at the beginning of the twentieth century could have foretold that, within a decade or more, Middle Eastern oil, Malayan rubber, and North American machine tools were to become vital to British military effort. And few could have predicted that within two decades the security of an Empire based on command of the surface of the sea was no longer assured. At the end of the nineteenth century, Admiral Mahan was still contending that command of the sea was identical with world power, but by the time that Alcock and Brown had flown their fragile craft across the Atlantic in 1919, his dictum—which had been confirmed by the test of history since the days of the Armada—had lost its unconditional validity.[2]

Between 1914 and 1918, thanks to the American alliance, the German menace was dissipated, although there were moments in 1917 when the scales seemed to balance precariously. The victory, when it came, was decisive, but the narrowness of the safety margin was never fully appreciated either in Britain or in the Dominions. Indeed, the sudden collapse of Germany, followed by the humiliating scuttling of her High Seas fleet in Scapa Flow, served to conceal the fundamental economic transformations that were steadily whittling away Britain's traditional supremacy as an imperial power. By the thirties, when both Germany and Japan began to re-arm on a large scale, their industries had developed to a point that enabled them to win a clear head-start over their quiescent and impoverished imperial rival. By 1939 Britain had neither the industrial capacity, nor the raw materials, nor the manpower, to compete successfully in an arms race with Germany and Japan. Both Britain and France, as subsequent events were to reveal, continued to be dependent on the resources of the United States.

2. G. S. Graham, *Empire of the North Atlantic*, 2nd ed. (London and Toronto, 1958), p. 311.

In these circumstances, unstinted military cooperation on the part of the British Dominions could not have provided more than feather counterweight to the expanding armament industries of aggressive powers seeking more *Lebensraum*. With the exception of Canada, the Dominions had in the past made contributions of ships and money to the Royal Navy, but the feeling of separate nationality which had developed steadily in the years before 1914 blocked any scheme of joint imperial defence. As a problem of naval strategy alone, it was obvious that the most economical and efficient defence lay in a single navy under one command, but the political aspect can never be ignored. In surrendering, as the Admiralty had done in 1909, the principle of central command for the whole Empire, the British government were simply submitting to the inevitable—viz., the uncompromising national mood of the Dominions.

In the years after 1918, the Dominions had advanced into a hard world as independent, self-governing nations, without, however, making any serious effort to become self-defending. After the Peace, Canada promptly discarded her newly-created war industries, becoming in consequence almost as dependent upon outside supply as Gambia or Hong Kong. In 1923 and 1926 Imperial Conferences asserted the principle that each part of the Empire was primarily responsible for its own local defence. Yet by the latter year, with the exception of Australia, none of the Dominions was buying or building war vessels to safeguard its own ports and sea lanes. Not until 1928 did the Canadian government borrow two destroyers from the British Admiralty, and arrange for the purchase of two more for delivery in 1931.

Too close an involvement in British military affairs, it was urged, meant danger to status and the risk of embroilment in foreign wars. In Ottawa, it was argued that Canada should continue to cut her commitments inside the Commonwealth. A British bloc, declared the prime minister, W. L. Mackenzie King, would excite resentful opposition throughout the world. In brief, a curious isolationist reaction against the erstwhile dominant British Empire developed during the inter-war years. In Canada especially, during the thirties, the denigration of Empire and the condemnation of militarists became as fashionable a university exercise as in Oxford. Nationalism was expressed with the negative pomposity of the cynic, whose Common Room sophistries ignored the world the brown locusts were already beginning to devour.

Happily for the safety and comfort of the major Dominions, the First World War had paved the way for the entrenchment of a principle of British policy that had already been accepted in spirit, namely, that the new English-speaking world power, the United States, should never again be considered as a potential enemy. But the new entente had its drawbacks. On American insistence, the old Japanese alliance of 1902 was abandoned to make way for the Washington Treaty of 1922, which confirmed Japanese naval supremacy in the Pacific. The British position in the East was now dependent on Japanese goodwill, which British governments for ten years tried assiduously and anxiously to cultivate. Admittedly, the agreed fleet ratios (5–5–3) left Japan inferior to Britain and the United States in total tonnage, but the absolute reduction in both the British and the American fleets left neither power strong enough to compete with Japan in eastern waters. The European equilibrium which had supported a Pax Britannica for the world during the nineteenth century, had disintegrated. In 1897 Britain stood apparently secure and unthreatened by any power; by 1939 she confronted highly industrialized powers east and west without being able to draw substantial supplementary support from either colonies or Dominions.

Once again a world war was won, and for a brief

moment the imperial pattern seemed, superficially, to be not very different from what it had been in 1919. It was soon evident, however, that forces had been unleashed which no quality of statecraft could stem. Initiated by Japanese conquests, new, inflammatory compulsions originating in national and racial self-consciousness shattered the imperial ramparts in southeast Asia, sending sympathetic waves of almost equal violence in the direction of Africa. Unlike the growth of nationalism in the older Dominions, the transition towards political autonomy came with an explosive suddenness. Nationalism has always been a separative force, but the exigencies of the Second World War stimulated an awakening in some respects reminiscent of the French Revolution. However unprepared they were for the entire responsibilities of self-government, the so-called backward or under-developed peoples were determined to put an end to their British tutelage. The day of benevolent trusteeship was over; government by ordered constitutional evolution was rudely deposed from its place at the centre of administrative practice. Within a decade after the end of the Second World War, a nation which had colonized almost a third of the world and built an Empire greater than the Romans had renounced its ancient heritage.

Imperial rule was quickly terminated in India, where the war had interrupted decades of over-cautious experiment. The constitutional turning-point came in 1949, following the division of the subcontinent into Pakistan and India. By means of a simple formula, the new Asian Dominions were able to accept the idea of an Empire turned Commonwealth, because the old obligation of allegiance to the Crown, upon which the original imperial structure had been based, was abandoned. The final solution was to accept India—and six years later, Pakistan—as republics which acknowledged the King as Head of the Commonwealth.

It was a startling concession, but at least the new arrangement did recognize the unique position of the Crown as the only institution essential to the Commonwealth relationship. The monarchy was to remain—even though in a diminished sense—a unifying symbol, and not just the Royal emblem of territories peopled by British stock. Nonetheless, the Crown was no longer common to the association as one juristic being, and its reduction was, in fact, to diminish the substance and significance of the Commonwealth itself. The symbol remained (and it is still important as a symbol), but relationships among republican nations no longer fell within the realm of British constitutional law. Not that there is anything sacrosanct about the British legal and parliamentary system. On the other hand, it is difficult to contemplate an enduring Commonwealth which includes members who may reject the heritage of peculiar freedoms guaranteed under British law. The extent to which the rule of law is sustained by parliamentary practice in India could have tremendous significance for the rest of the Commonwealth. If India can combine an Indian style of politics, wrote Professor Dennis Austin, with the substance of constitutional government, "then it may be that other countries in other parts of the Commonwealth will find a way of combining their nationalist desire for innovation with their legacies from colonial rule."[3]

Meanwhile, the record of success in transferring sovereign power to Indians, Pakistanis, and Ceylonese had made Whitehall optimistic that the African colonies might share the happy consummation. In Africa there appeared to be time to meet the new and unprecedented challenge. At the moment when India and Pakistan were embarking

3. *Commonwealth Journal*, XI (December 1968), 247.

on their careers as republics, the four West African territories of Nigeria, the Gold Coast, Sierra Leone, and Gambia were still governed as colonies and protectorates, with powers vested in governors assisted by executive and legislative councils. Despite the extensive devolution of local responsibilities to legislative councils and Native Authorities, effective control remained with British officials. Given another decade of reasonable tranquillity, the transfer to independence might have been negotiated in some comfort.

Unfortunately, at a time when constitutional advance in the shape of unofficial majorities in the legislature had already outrun popular political development, the floodgates of African nationalism blew open. The most liberal and carefully constructed programmes could not ensure the cooperation of colonial leaders exposed to, and not infrequently inebriated by, the heady wine of post-war nationalism. Beginning in West Africa, by 1951 the "New Deal" of the 1940s had been overtaken by the same waves of emotion that had earlier overwhelmed India and Burma. The ideal of partnership between British colonial governments and African peoples, somewhat optimistically promulgated before the war, rapidly disintegrated under the attacks of African politicians, who saw "equal partnership" as not more than a subtle scheme for keeping Europeans in power.

In fact, a single decade witnessed the almost total withdrawal of European imperial rule in tropical areas of the world. During that brief period, over thirty African colonies gained their independence. The process, starting with Ghana's attainment of internal self-government in 1951 as the prelude to independence in 1957, was completed in July 1968 with the passing of the Swaziland Independence Bill. Excepting Rhodesia, which has occupied an anomalous position since 1923, and apart from the island dependencies of St. Helena and the Seychelles, the

British withdrawal is complete. Today seven-eighths of the present Commonwealth population consists of Asians and Africans, and more than half of the member-states are Asian or African republics.

Some critics have suggested that the British succumbed too soon to the intense demands of nationalism, and that beneficent delays might have worked to the advantage of the former colonies. Certainly, Britain was capable of holding on longer, at least west of Suez, without unduly straining her military or economic resources. But considering the ethos of the 1950s, use of imperial *force majeure* was out of the question. British public opinion would not, by that time, have tolerated the expensive imposition of indefinite rule by force of arms on unwilling populations.[4]

On the other hand, it has been submitted that this post-war surrender of empire was a consequence of weariness, weakness, and a growing ineptitude. Admittedly, the will to stay the course had been sapped by the enervating sacrifices of war, especially in the eastern areas overrun by the Japanese. Yet such an argument ignores the fact that during the fifties attainment of independence was regarded as appropriate fulfilment. To many British people, it was not a humiliating defeat, comparable to the loss of the Thirteen Colonies in 1783, but a meritorious enlargement of the Commonwealth. In this sense, history contributed to naïveté. Concessions under pressure of colonial nationalism had been made repeatedly since Lord Durham's day without loss of face or enduring regrets. The premature birth of several independent Asian and African nations was a little frightening, but their appearance meant no drastic break in the historic continuity of the imperial household. The evolution of the old British Empire towards auton-

4. See A. J. Hanna, "The British Retreat from Empire," in *Britain and the Netherlands in Europe and Asia*, ed. J. S. Bromley and E. H. Kossman (London, 1968), p. 235.

omy and equality could still be regarded as a process leading inevitably to a Commonwealth, reconstructed and modernized, but without loss of structural stability.

In fact, however, the British government had been caught up almost unawares by "winds of change." The years of gradual constitutional evolution were past, and ministers prepared to run, before the storm reached hurricane force. Up to the moment when Mr. Macmillan adopted what mid-Victorian imperialists would have called a policy of "scuttle,"[5] British official emphasis had been concentrated on preparedness for the responsibilities of full self-government. As it happened, by 1960 Britain was already on her way out of West Africa, with Belgium and France following close behind.

Thenceforward, there was to be no benevolent transfer of power, only a shaking-off of responsibilities. The African colonies had suddenly become encumbrances to be got rid of as quickly as possible. By 1961 even the man on the street was becoming aware that his Empire, like the Hollander's some ten years earlier, was on the slippery slope, and that official brakes had been removed. During and after the public debate over South African membership in the Commonwealth (concluding with South Africa's departure) the increasingly sensitive national conscience was shaken by irresponsible blasts from the Trusteeship Council of the United Nations, whose demagogues inveighed against the evils of "colonialism."[6] At the same time, many British journalists and academics prepared to exorcise the word "imperialism" as a symbol of past shame, thus helping to infect the British public with a

5. The "Winds of Change" speech (3 February 1960) is contained in Nicholas Mansergh, *Documents and Speeches on Commonwealth Affairs 1952–1962* (London, 1963), pp. 347–51.

6. See in this connection, Robin W. Winks, *Failed Federations: Decolonization and the British Empire* (University of Nottingham, Cust Foundation Lecture 1970), pp. 17–19.

guilt complex that is not easily erased. It was a dismal finale to an era of empire. Both government and people were unprepared, not for the event as a probable development, but for the suddenness of the transition from dependence to autonomy.

Without doubt, the saddest feature of the retreat was the speed of withdrawal. West and East Africa were the outstanding examples of precipitate action. In 1948 violent demonstrations had prompted the despatch of the Aitken-Watson Commission to the Gold Coast, and their report led to the granting of internal self-government. A campaign headed by Dr. Nkruma, demanding further constitutional surrenders, culminated in the grant of independence in 1957, the territory taking the barely appropriate name of Ghana as a full member of the Commonwealth. The stage was thus set for the other three West African territories. The Eastern and Western regions of Nigeria were granted internal self-government in 1957, and the largely Moslem Northern region in 1959, within the framework of a federation which achieved control of its own destinies in 1960, only to face seven years later the ghastly tragedy of civil war. Sierra Leone obtained responsible government in 1958, and thenceforward pressed strongly for independence which was granted in April 1961. In Gambia, consitutional progress was less rapid; yet a large measure of control in domestic affairs soon passed into the hands of Africans, and independence came in 1965.

Meanwhile, the speed and decisiveness of change in the far less sophisticated communities of British East Africa was, if possible, even more unexpected. In 1957 few if any would have predicted the constitutional revolution in Kenya, or that Tanganyika and Uganda would be heading for full self-government and independence. Tanganyika became internally self-governing early in 1961 and membership as a separate nation within the Commonwealth came in the same year; Uganda followed in 1962. Zanzibar reached a similar goal in December 1963, an event which was shortly followed by a bloody coup d'état, the establishment of a People's Republic, and shortly afterwards union with Tanganyika.[7] In all three East African states, representation by Europeans was permitted, and in Kenya actually exists (subject to vulnerable safeguards), but political power has passed completely into African hands, a precipitate transition which ended an anomalous and largely untenable state of racial partnership in government.

Today, suspicion and bitterness, some of it invoked by doctrinaire enthusiasts in the name of multi-racialism, cloud the air of Commonwealth conference halls. The old fraternity of white Dominions has ended. Yet it would be ridiculous to claim that diminishing confidence in, and enthusiasm for, the Commonwealth in Great Britain is simply a matter of the "white club" being borne down in a tide of fashionable colour. The admission of African and Asian members hastened but it did not initiate a process of disillusionment that had already begun with the imminent demise of the old Empire, revealing itself in the first cautious attentions to the European Community.

The significant fact about the reorganized Commonwealth is not that the membership is largely non-white, but that it is non-Anglo-Saxon in origin. The real and deep-rooted differences have nothing to do with skin-tincture; they are racial, and in that sense cultural; and while, no doubt, they may in time be eradicable, I cannot

7. In 1968, Chinese Communists were making a considerable effort to establish a beachhead at Dar-es-Salaam. It was not only a matter of running arms; some seven hundred Chinese experts, chiefly engineers and technicians, entered the country. Happily, fears that China would use Tanganyika and especially Zanzibar as bases for the general infiltration of Africa have subsided, largely owing to President Nyerere's political sense.

see the antipathies or misunderstandings which they nourish dissolving in the near future. There have of course been brave challenges by the politically wary and the pretentious, but neither the self-indulgent righteousness of Lord Caradon and Mr. Lester Pearson, nor the crusading zeal of the World Council of Churches, is likely to generate the magic necessary to promote social and racial integration within a Commonwealth association.

Admittedly, French-Canadians, Afrikaners, and southern Irish were in the old days equally outside the generic pale. But they were of European stock, and in numbers hardly likely to "rock the boat." By the sixties, the sudden and heavy reinforcements of non-British independent states tipped the balance irretrievably against any British-dominated or British-infused type of association. As a result, although a common *lingua franca* was still available, members found difficulty in speaking the same political language—unless, as at prime ministers' conferences, they indulged in double-talk. Values once cherished (without neglect of self-interest) were either neutralized by dilution or disregarded as politically too awkward to sustain. Some of the less-developed countries found it difficult to uphold particular standards of political freedom and administration once regarded as essential to the old family alliance.

In these days, corruption and lack of discipline represent dangers to domestic health and Commonwealth stability which it is impossible to over-emphasize. Moreover, in some member states there has been a denial of certain rights like individual freedom under the law which were formerly regarded as fundamental. After the withdrawal of South Africa, it was suggested that the Commonwealth had acquired a new moral purpose. But such evanescent idealism as may have been evoked during this brief crisis was not sufficient to mend the breach between India and Pakistan or to stop civil war in Nigeria, nor did Commonwealth ties serve to lessen the conflict between Greek and

Turk in Cyprus, between Malay and Chinese in Malaysia, or Muslim and Hindu in East Pakistan.

In short, the old British Empire had failed to blossom into the elegant and stately edifice that optimists had anticipated. Must we then accept the unpalatable truth and admit that the traditional effort to graft western political institutions on alien cultures was mistaken policy, or that parliamentary government was unsuited for, or at least unworkable in, most of the new Commonwealth nations? Was it reasonable to expect that peculiarly British institutions could develop roots in oriental and African lands, where transfer of ideas and practices was subject to the influence of differing climate, social structure, and hereditary custom?

Recently, I happened to pick up the diary and letters of a young pre-1914 political officer, Lieutenant Arnold Wilson, a Kiplingesque hero who in many respects represented a generation which could scarcely have existed without the Empire.[8] At the age of twenty-four, he surveyed and helped to secure for Great Britain the forbidding area of the first great oil concessions adjoining the Persian Gulf. With a maturity beyond his years, he soaked up the political ethos of Persia and her neighbours, and came to the conclusion that "Parliaments are not for the East and we shall do an ill turn to India if we introduce Parliamentary institutions. Everyone is talking about them . . . they are the modern road of ambitious men to power and wealth,

8. Sir Arnold Wilson, *S.W. Persia, Letters and Diary of a Young Political Officer* (London, 1942). One of the last acts of Wilson's incredibly varied career was to join the Royal Air Force in October 1939, at the age of fifty-five. It was characteristic of the man to refuse (as he told his constituents of Hitchen, an electoral division which he had represented since 1933) to shelter himself behind the bodies of young men. As an air-gunner serving with No. 37 squadron, he was shot down in the course of operations over the Dunkirk area on the night of 31 May 1940.

but they will never take root in this soil or anywhere East of Suez—indeed I sometimes doubt if they will even take root East of the English Channel and the North Sea."[9]

It would be difficult to prove that parliamentary institutions are intrinsically unsuited either to the Asian or the African mentality. On the other hand, without a politically conscious middle-class from which to recruit year by year the operators of such institutions, the transfer of such apparatus to India and Africa was bound to carry great risks. Without a constant replenishing estate, such as existed in Great Britain and in some of the Dominions, the practice of parliamentary government was likely to be spasmodic and precarious. There were of course small cadres of professionals in all the colonies. Up to the fifties training in the Westminster manner had been provided for handfuls of politicians and civil servants. But they were too few, and the reservoir of talent on which they might draw was too small. Indeed, not until the latter days of the old Empire was the colonial admitted as an equal into the civil service. Consequently, when explosive nationalism hurtled him across a century of western experience within a decade, he was obviously not qualified for all the political responsibilities of independence.

Basically, parliamentary democracy depends for existence on a substantial electorate, protected from the power of the state by strong voluntary associations, and intelligent and sensitive enough to distinguish between sane and foolish leadership, and between humane and corrupt administration. In not all the former colonies could these conditions have been met. On the other hand, whatever the deficiencies, the leaders of the self-same colonies were determined, when the time came, to have nothing less than the precise "mirror and transcript" of the British constitution (to use the language of the Younger Pitt when

9. Letter to his father, 1908; ibid., p. 44.

he described the Canada Act of 1791), and this attitude was accepted automatically in Great Britain. Deeply concerned about concepts of individual liberty and law, British statesmen tended to regard any drastic alternative with uneasiness if not with horror. Sure in their faith, they failed to appreciate that the glittering Westminster chalice, presented with pride and honest warmth, could be poisoned.

Paradoxically, the danger was inherent in the very machinery that was expected to function in the interests of popular liberties. A compound engine cannot be made to work efficiently on one cylinder. In Africa, chiefly as a result of the heat generated by independence movements, strong opposition parties failed to take shape. Yet, as in Britain, parliament remained the absolute sovereign, and the real substance of power lay with the executive through parliament. Consequently, to take one example, by exercising in perfectly legal fashion the unrestricted powers of parliament over an illiterate electorate that had voted away its freedom, Kwame Nkruma was able to set up his dictatorship in Ghana. In the words of Tanzania's President, Julius Nyerere, the Westminster model, depending for its effectiveness on the two-party system, was "a positive invitation to tyranny."

Although it is dangerous to dogmatize, in retrospect it would seem likely that most emerging Asian and African states would have found a presidential form of government with strong executive powers more appropriate. Certainly the idea of a one-party monolithic state seemed to be growing in favour, until in Pakistan, and more recently in Ghana, Nigeria, and Sierra Leone, it was replaced by military rule. Generally speaking, politics is a civilian art demanding considerable professional skill, and army officers have not always proved themselves competent to carry out the civil responsibilities which they have pre-empted or had thrust upon them. But at the present stage of development it is not unreasonable to suppose that a Sandhurst graduate may prove quite as useful as a professional party politician. History teaches us that most of the nastiest dictators have been civilians, not soldiers.

Reduced in terms of kinship unity, and consequently weakened in importance as a collective world force, the Commonwealth remains today a loose association of unequal partners, some sophisticated, others less mature, some rich, some poor, some viable, many insecure. Collaboration based on convenience and self-interest is probably the only cement that holds them together. On the other hand, one must not ignore the fact that British rule was for many years, indeed in Asia for centuries, a vital phase of colonial life. Inevitably history stamped a rough mould of common interests, combining language, commercial and legal practice, and many of the ordinary humdrum ways of life. Only time will tell whether member states will break completely from these patterns interwoven as they are with sentiment as well as habit.

In these unsettled times, the growing pains of nationalism may well mask the existence of such legacies. Yet righteous objectives and honest rule can scarcely be presented as a justification for unimaginative administration. British colonial policy prior to the Second World War was too much a matter of drift, of meeting the needs of the day as they came. Ministers, colonial office officials, and governors tended to assess imperial problems in the light of past experience, reducing them to traditional formulae often irrelevant in the light of contemporary conditions. There was insufficient attention to the historical and geographical background of primitive or under-developed colonies, their economic potential, and their capacities to produce a politically educated élite, so essential as a basis of self-government. There was little effort during what might be called the advanced training stages to move away from the worn-out mould of constitutional evolution.

Moreover, the day by day controls of Empire were sometimes in the hands of the ignorant and the indifferent, of men insensitive to the cultural life and aspirations of the peoples they governed. Against this, however, it must be said that British rule was rarely in the hands of the cruel and unscrupulous. British colonial servants were sometimes smug and arrogant, and occasionally in danger of being throttled by the old school tie. But perhaps the more important fact is how very few were corrupted or de-civilized by the power they administered. The playing fields of Eton may have produced many rigid and unsympathetic characters, but few saw themselves as gods, entrusted with shaping the character and destinies of other human beings. The least lovable and the most inept were usually rigorous in their efforts to uphold British civil service standards, and judging by letters and diaries, the best of them found deep satisfaction in serving backward peoples in some of the unhealthiest parts of the globe. More than that, they developed a strong sense of duty and loyalty to the varied races they governed—an affection particularly for the unsophisticated innocent or underdog.

All told, it was an association that was cherished at the time, and which has, generally speaking, stood the test of succeeding violent years. These proconsuls may have held views on the meaning of empire very different from our own, but this does not mean that they were a narrow, self-centred lot, whose minds had been nurtured on insular creeds and schoolboy dogmas. Some were talented explorers and archaeologists; some were scholars of distinguished quality; a few were superb statesmen. Without doubt their form of colonial rule was responsible for injuries to pride and person that healed but slowly. On the other hand, their work must be judged not only in the light of a glorious liberation from the bondage of "colonialism," but against the dark background of political corruption, tribal factionalism, and even, on occasion, of starvation and massacre which independence brought in its wake. Looking backward from the confusion of our own times, from a world racked by conflict and tension, one is granted a perspective of empire that dilutes or dissolves any pangs of self-reproach. Indeed, one might hazard that the peoples whom the Empire-builders once served gained more than they lost from British dominion overseas.